The Flexible Lyric

The Life of Poetry
POETS ON THEIR ART AND CRAFT

ELLEN BRYANT VOIGT

The Flexible Lyric

THE UNIVERSITY OF GEORGIA PRESS

ATHENS AND LONDON

Published by the University of Georgia Press
Athens, Georgia 30602
© 1999 by Ellen Bryant Voigt
All rights reserved
Designed by Erin Kirk New and Betty Palmer McDaniel
Set in 10 on 13 Fairfield Medium
by G & S Typesetters, Inc.
Printed and bound by McNaughton & Gunn, Inc.
The paper in this book meets the guidelines for
permanence and durability of the Committee on
Production Guidelines for Book Longevity of the
Council on Library Resources.

Printed in the United States of America
03 02 01 00 99   P   5 4 3 2 1

Library of Congress Cataloging-in-Publication Data
Voigt, Ellen Bryant, 1943–
    The flexible lyric / by Ellen Bryant Voigt.
        p.   cm. — (The life of poetry: poets on their art
    and craft)
    Includes bibliographical references and index.
    ISBN 0-8203-2131-1 (pbk. : alk. paper)
    1. Voigt, Ellen Bryant, 1943–   —Authorship.
    2. Poetry—Authorship.   3. Poetics.   I. Title.   II. Series.
    PS3572.O34Z466   1999
    808.1—dc21   99-24808

British Library Cataloging-in-Publication Data available

Contents

Acknowledgments

All but two of these pieces began as lectures, and I have assumed for this book the original audience: serious students of the craft of poetry. More important, all the pieces owe their existence to the Warren Wilson College MFA Writing Program, where I teach. Often I was exploring issues raised within that community's ongoing conversation, or trying to add a writer's perspective to the existing body of scholarship; always the arguments I develop here were tried out there first and strengthened by rigorous opposition or generous support. Before and after such airings I also counted heavily on the intelligence and wisdom of Stephen Dobyns, Louise Glück, Lorrie Goldensohn, Donald Hall, James Longenbach, Heather McHugh, Gregory Orr, and Michael Ryan. In addition, Ruth Anderson Barnett, Kurt Brown, David Fenza, T. R. Hummer, and Dave Smith scrupulously attended to the transformation from podium to page.

The idea for a book began five years ago, and with it began the three-part title essay on structure, which forms the heart of the volume. It is my presumption, explicit there and implicit elsewhere, that lyric is what most of us are writing these days when we write in lines, narrative and drama having been more happily advanced in prose; and it is my intention to counter our own genre-resistance—sometimes even genre-deprecation—by refuting directly or indirectly some of the current restricted notions of what the lyric has been and can be.

It should be noted that drafts of Elizabeth Bishop's "One Art" are printed with permission from Special Collections, Vassar College Libraries; the estate of Elizabeth Bishop; and Farrar, Straus and Giroux. I am also grateful to Frank Bidart for his log on draft 15.

Finally, I thank those editors who published versions of these essays under the following titles: "A Moment's Thought," in *Southern Indiana Review*, was reprinted in *Facing The Lion: Writers on Life and Craft*, ed. Kurt Brown (Boston: Beacon, 1996); "Image" appeared in *New England Review* and was reprinted in *Poets Teaching Poets: Self and the World*, eds. Gregory Orr and Ellen Bryant Voigt (Ann Arbor: University of Michigan Press, 1996); "In Defense of the Lyric: Point of View" and "Narrative and Lyric: Structural Subversion" in *Southern Review*; "In The Waiting Room," *AWP Chronicle*; "On Tone," *New England Review and Breadloaf Quarterly*; "Poetic Structure: The Flexible Lyric" and "Poetry and Gender," *Kenyon Review*.

In the Waiting Room

In Oxford, Mississippi, having cruised Main Street, going (as Benjy did not) the correct legal way around the square and its Confederate soldier, you make your way to William Faulkner's house, "Rowanoak," set back from the street imposingly in a grove of large old trees. Don't ask which tree is a "rowan oak": a rowan is an ash, "rowan oak" not a species like "live oak" or "white oak" or "pinoak" but more like the "u" he inserted in his name; more like his portrait, in oils, in full riding habit, as if riding to the hounds *were* his habit; more like the widow's-walk balcony he had built on, which is, in fact, inaccessible to widows or anyone else inside the house.

Inside: a curator on duty; leatherbound sets in the parlor where the portrait hangs; Robert Lowell's inscription in *Lord Weary's Castle*—"to our greatest living writer"; *Homage to Mistress Bradstreet* with Ben Shahn illustrations and John Berryman's mash note on the title page, alternately fawning and imperious. In the tiny back room: cot, bookshelf, typewriter, and, written on the wall, a yellowed outline of *The Fable*. This last was discovered in renovation to be already preserved for the ages— the hand that held the pen may also have wielded the shellac. On the way out, pick up a literary map of the town; the prototypes for the Yoknapatawpha mansions help explain the pretensions of

"Rowanoak," fame and money lifting the foot to a higher rung on the local social ladder.

Looking closely at a hero's mortal parts has always been a risky enterprise. We want our great writers pure of heart—or think we do, ignoring that unattractive *frisson* we feel learning otherwise. There was, for instance, much noisy clucking over Philip Larkin's published correspondence and the vitriol therein, even though the poems had long before suggested the larger condition, a misanthropy that included everyone, people of any gender or ethnicity and most particularly himself. The authority accorded Lawrance Thompson's view of Frost, only now being withdrawn somewhat, may demonstrate how thoroughly we've accepted W. B. Yeats's dictum—that one cannot perfect both the life and the art—and how we take cover in it as unavoidable choice, an ethical loophole, the hazard in the vocation. Never mind that for Yeats it *was* a choice, but between the activist and the poet, energies spent on a national literature or on his own. Meanwhile, we seldom importune good-citizen minor poets with the same fervor.

Meanwhile, too, since we are lacking biographical detail (her mother and now her aunt have been stringent executors), Flannery O'Connor's status as hero and icon remains ambiguous. There are the major achievements, which anyone would wish for; and the restricted life, which no one would; and the presumed simplistic relationship between them that we, well, envy, crossing ourselves—as if the suffering were the cost of the work or even the cause of the work, prison being after all a focused solitude. And there are the enforced wit in the letters, the grim look of the photographs, the undisclosed sexuality, the passionate religious faith: enough for either a shrine or an exposé at the end of any ambivalent pilgrimage.

Houses with names always seem to petition grandeur, and "Andalusia" is where O'Connor lived out her short adult life and wrote all her mature fiction. "Country place" is the descriptor used by Robert Giroux, her New York editor; in New England, executives and academics often have a "house in the country" to which they repair for weekends and summers. In parts of the South, "country house" may suggest even greater privilege, the antebellum family estate—"Rowanoak" with acreage—and O'Connor, unlike Faulkner, was born to property and lineage.

To get there, I took a county hardtop a few miles out of Milledgeville, Georgia, opened a gate in the barbed wire fence, and turned into the dirt farm road. Rather than set into woods, the house has a few trees squared up to it, more functional than decorative, and it is small in any case: a bungalow, decidedly postbellum, enclosed front porch, a row of dormer windows over that like eyebrows grown together. Thirty years after her death at thirty-nine there was a pump in the side yard, on a concrete slab, and padlocks on all the doors. The yard, carved out of the pasture, was patchy from the shade trees; trying to imagine it with free-range peacocks, parody of both royal excess and rural poverty, I remembered O'Connor's gift for self-mockery, and now remember this too: an Andalusian is a kind of chicken. Andalusia must be the tenant's house.

By the early 1950s in rural Piedmont a shrewd independent farmer could make enough on high-yield, low-acreage crops, and livestock, for a two-bedroom brick house and a John Deere tractor to replace the mule. Preferring something like Faulkner's bipolar arrangement of cultured but decadent Compsons and pragmatic but barbaric Snopeses—something like a fraying Hunt Club on the one hand, chickens in the front yard on the other—rigid southeastern society withstood as long as possible this emerging lower-middle class. Even after the disintegration of plantation economy, the romance of aristocracy tried to keep a sharp division between those who worked with their hands and those who hired those who worked with their hands. Land owned by banks or speculators was usually farmed by sharecroppers, who took a portion of the yield, sometimes under mortgage agreements that eventually purchased the land with labor. What remained of land-grant estates, whoever now owned them or pieces of them, was usually farmed by "tenants": a family, white or black, lived in a house provided by the landowner, maintained the farm, and supervised day laborers (usually black) brought in to help plant and harvest. The result was a complex, subdivided social hierarchy.

A representative census can be found in the doctor's waiting room in O'Connor's story "Revelation":

> Next to the ugly girl was the child . . . and next to him was a thin leathery old woman in a cotton print dress. She and Claud had three sacks of chicken feed in their pump house that was in the same print. She had seen from the first that the child belonged with the old woman. She could tell by the way they sat—kind of vacant and white-trashy. . . . [N]ext to the well-dressed pleasant lady was a lank-faced woman who was certainly the child's mother. She had on a yellow sweat-shirt and wine-colored slacks, both gritty-looking, and the rims of her lips were stained with snuff. Her dirty yellow hair was tied with a little piece of red paper ribbon. . . .
>
> Next to the child's mother was a red-headed youngish woman, reading one of the magazines and working a piece of chewing gum. . . . She was not white-trash, just common. Sometimes Mrs. Turpin occupied herself at night naming the classes of people. On the bottom of the heap were most colored people, not the kind she would have been if she had been one, but most of them; then next to them—not above, just away from—were the white-trash; then above them were the home-owners, and above them the home-and-land owners, to which she and Claud belonged. Above she and Claud were people with a lot of money and much bigger houses and much more land. But here the complexity of it would begin to bear in on her, for some of the people with a lot of money were common and ought to be below she and Claud and some of the people who had good blood had lost their money and had to rent and then there were colored people who owned their homes and land as well. There was a colored

dentist in town who had two red Lincolns and a swimming pool and a farm with registered white-face cattle on it. Usually by the time she had fallen sleep all the classes of people were moiling and roiling around in her head.

What O'Connor gets exactly right is the economic roots of bigotry. And she gets the tone right, too, when smugness undermines grammar (*above* and *below she and Claud*, Mrs. Turpin says).

O'Connor insisted on two crucial elements in fiction, mystery and manners, terms she borrowed from Henry James: "the mystery of our position on earth, and . . . those conventions which, in the hands of the artist, reveal that central mystery . . . embodied in the concrete world of sense experience. . . . You get the manners from the texture of existence that surrounds you." An only child, she was born in Savannah in 1925, and moved, at twelve, when her father was gravely ill, to Milledgeville, birthplace of her mother, Regina Cline O'Connor. Her father died when Flannery was fifteen, and the two survivors lived on, as Sally Fitzgerald notes, "in the fine old home of the Cline family." After high school she attended Georgia State College for Women in the same town; by the time she received her degree in 1945, "she knew very well what she could and wanted to do" (*The Habit of Being*).

Meaning: she took herself "away," to the Iowa Writers Workshop, to Yaddo, briefly to New York City, then to the Fitzgeralds in Connecticut, meanwhile exchanging with Regina almost daily letters (which Regina withheld from Fitzgerald's published collection). In December 1950, O'Connor left on the train for Christmas and arrived home desperately ill. After lengthy hospitalizations, remissions, one last summer "up north," then the diagnosis of lupus, she came back to stay and moved with her mother out to the farm—according to Giroux, because O'Connor could no longer climb stairs. The letters are characteristically breezy on the point, like this one written in September 1951: "Me & Maw are still at the farm and are like to be, I perceive, through the winter. She is nuts about it out here, surrounded by the low-ing herd and other details, and considers it beneficial to my health."

Like Elizabeth Bishop's steam shovel, "awful but cheerful" is the picture that emerges of Regina. Flannery was hospitalized of-ten, and at home she required daily shots of ACTH, a volatile, de-bilitating steroid. The move out of town, out of easy reach of neighbors and doctors, must have been an economic decision, as the earlier move from Savannah back to Milledgeville may have been. For evidence there is, in O'Connor's letters, a recurring fix-ation on money—contracts, royalties, stipends, whether checks had arrived as promised, when they would arrive. It runs like a ground note under "the habit of being," the life O'Connor made willfully of discipline, faith, hardship, hard work, and good hu-mor. And it suggests a real if profane parallel to the "Catholic themes" she was always asked about: "The things we see, hear, smell and touch affect us long before we believe anything at all. . . . [O]ur senses have responded irrevocably to a certain re-ality. . . . What the . . . writer is apt to find, when he descends within his imagination, is the life . . . in which he is both native and alien. He discovers that the imagination is not free, but bound" (*Mystery and Manners*).

Age twelve is plenty old enough to have registered the central family drama. Edward Francis O'Connor's illness (probably also lupus) and death had made Regina dependent on the home folks; despite her daughter's appetite for travel, intelligence, and ambi-tion, the sleepy little college just down the street must have been the only feasible option. Now, with unending medical bills again, the move from town. It is plausible that Regina felt keenly that she had "come down in the world" from the impressive resi-dences in Milledgeville and Savannah, a trajectory intriguing in its parallel to the central Christian lesson and to her daughter's repeated use, in her fiction, of experience that humbles—in such strong contradiction, say, to Faulkner's impulse to ennoble. Meanwhile, it's awfully hard NOT to see Regina incarnated in Mrs. Turpin, in Julian's oblivious mother ("Everything That Rises

Must Converge"), or in the nitwit grandmother ("A Good Man Is Hard to Find"). And hard not to see unflinching self-portraits by Flannery in Julian, in Hulga marooned in the hayloft, or in

> a fat girl of eighteen or nineteen, scowling into a thick blue book which Mrs. Turpin saw was entitled *Human Develop-ment*. The girl raised her head and directed her scowl at Mrs. Turpin as if she did not like her looks. She appeared annoyed that anyone should speak while she tried to read. The poor girl's face was blue with acne and Mrs. Turpin thought how pitiful it was to have a face like that at any age. She gave the girl a friendly smile but the girl only scowled the harder.

The ugly girl will be the agent of the "revelation," beaning Mrs. Turpin with the book and prompting the devastating vision out at the hog pens, but there's not a thing *likable* about her. On the other hand, a complicated empathy attaches, by the end of the stories, to the befuddled older character, to Julian's mother, to Mrs. Turpin gripped by the vision of souls "rumbling toward heaven,"

> shouting and clapping and leaping like frogs. And bringing up the end of the procession was a tribe of people whom she recognized at once as those who, like herself and Claud, had always had a little of everything and the God-given wit to use it right. She leaned forward to observe them closer. They were marching behind the others with great dignity, account-able as they had always been for good order and common sense and respectable behavior. They alone were on key. Yet she could see by their shocked and altered faces that even their virtues were being burned away.

Art, O'Connor said, "requires a delicate adjustment of the outer and inner worlds in such a way that, without changing their nature, they can be seen through each other. To know oneself is to know . . . the world, and it is also, paradoxically, a form of ex-ile from that world. . . . And to know oneself is, above all, to know what one lacks. It is to measure oneself against Truth, and not the other way around. The first product of self-knowledge is humility" (*Mystery and Manners*).

When I first read O'Connor, in 1961, I was a refugee from a Virginia town even smaller than Milledgeville, and relatives as immediate and more numerous, and an embarrassingly rural background. The embarrassment was new but acute, acquired quickly at a pedigreed women's college where I was a serious music student on scholarship. Dispensing with my freshman liberal arts requirement by way of a syllabus containing Faulkner, O'Connor, and other living writers, I actually wrote a published piece that year (published in the college magazine), a sort of long prose poem with hot biscuits and a slaughtered pig, but then filed it—and O'Connor—in a deep drawer. When I later moved irrevocably from music to poetry, it was by way of Herter Norton's Rainer Maria Rilke and W. B. Yeats—high rhetoric and lofty aesthetic—and about as far from the violent southern landscape, its sweaty religion, its shameful past, its tenant houses, as I could get. Then I also took myself "away."

It was from that self-selected exile that I came, in 1977, to a convention of writers—my first—in Washington, D.C., at a glittery hotel, hard by an embassy seized that weekend by Mideast terrorists. In the acre of plush that was the lobby a large vivid jungle bird blinked from its elaborate bamboo cage. The scribes, gathered for the Associated Writing Programs annual meeting, numbered something less than two hundred and had been assigned half a ballroom for the evening readings; the rest was packed with Automotive Body Paint Manufacturers, convened for a meal and a sales seminar. Through the temporary, corrugated partition came continual murmur punctuated by silverware-on-china and erratic applause. Our side was long, narrow, and flat, and the poet up front was short; past the fifth row of folding chairs one had to crane up out of one's seat for a clear look. From the general direction of matronly gray hair and square navy suit were emitted a few almost inaudible remarks—"man-moth" had been a newspaper misprint of "mammoth"—which slid imperceptibly into the texts of the poems, unmodulated.

Aside from one Vietnam protest where the second reader in nine held forth for an hour, and once when the poet was falling-down drunk, and once when the poems were simply execrable, as late as the spring of 1977 I'd not been to any "bad" readings. Which is to say, I still found each one thrilling for its public cele-bration, its return to the aural, its prurient pleasure in jacket-photo-come-alive, its sounded voice correcting past and future reading of the page. Freed into an associative buzz by an image, a rhyme scheme, an isolated memorable line, I had relished, as a lapsed musician, the difference in audience experience between a performance and a reading. Participatory solitude, I might have called the latter, something similar to "parallel play" in two-year-olds. But this time, it seemed, any music in the room would be what I supplied from memory, since the poet's characteristic iambic trimeter was overrun by the simple declarative syntax: she read as if from a newspaper the whole time. Having loved those poems, I determined not to listen.

James Merrill would describe, in his elegy for her (*New York Review of Books*, 1979), Elizabeth Bishop's "life-long imperson-ations of an ordinary woman," and her reading in Washington might be seen as a triumph of that persona. How long did it take me to register something else? Midway, when she switched to po-ems I didn't yet know from her new book (*Geography III*): I had no access to these texts except through that droning voice. What I had elevated in my silent reading was artifice, formal imposi-tions on natural syntax and common diction. What she made me hear—perhaps what she heard as she incised the poems onto the page, two a year—was idiom, one of the voices murmuring on the bus in Nova Scotia, "In the creakings and noises, / an old con-versation / —not concerning us, but recognizable,"

> names being mentioned, things cleared up finally; what he
> said, what she said, who got pensioned; deaths, deaths and

sicknesses; the year he remarried; the year (something) happened. She died in childbirth. . . . He took to drink. Yes. She
went to the bad. When Amos began to pray even in the store
and finally the family had to put him away. ". . . Life's like
that." ("The Moose")

Lightbulb over my head: *This isn't the music of song—it's the music of speech.* One might even call it, as O'Connor did, "manners,"
gotten "from the texture of existence," "the senses hav[ing] responded irrevocably to a certain reality"

> where a woman shakes a tablecloth
> out after supper.
>
> A pale flickering. Gone.
> The Tantramar marshes
> and the smell of salt hay.
> An iron bridge trembles
> and a loose plank rattles
> but doesn't give way.

Then Bishop had finished that poem and begun another, car-
rying on so thoroughly without me that I noticed neither the title
nor the opening lines, tuning in here:

> My island seemed to be a sort of cloud-dump. All the hemi-
> sphere's left-over clouds arrived and hung above the craters—
> their parched throats were hot to touch. Was that why it
> rained so much? And why sometimes the whole place hissed?
> The turtles lumbered by, high-domed, hissing like tea-
> kettles. . . . The folds of lava, running out to sea, would hiss.
> I'd turn. And then they'd prove to be more turtles. The
> beaches were all lava, variegated, black, red, and white, and
> gray; the marbled colors made a fine display.

What was the ghost-text this one was echoing? Something had
been triggered by that rhyme, and I chased down in memory this
passage:

The beach hisses like fat. On his left, a sheet
of interrupting water comes and goes
and glazes over his dark and brittle feet.
· ·
                     . . . As he runs,
he stares at the dragging grains. . . .
The millions of grains are black, white, tan, and gray,
mixed with quartz grains, rose and amethyst.

So the recent poem reprised the older one and confirmed its self-mocking *ars poetica*:

His beak is focussed; he is preoccupied,

looking for something, something, something.
Poor bird, he is obsessed!

                             ("Sandpiper")

But the poem she was reading hadn't stopped for my revelations and was moving to something new in the tone:

I often gave way to self-pity. . . . What's wrong with self-pity, anyway. . . . [T]he more pity I felt, the more I felt at home. . . . Dreams were the worst. . . . I'd have nightmares of other islands stretching away from mine, infinities of islands, islands spawning islands, like frogs' eggs turning into polliwogs of islands, knowing that I had to live on each and every one, eventually, for ages, registering their flora, their fauna, their geography.

So what had only been guessed at—that her "blood was full of them, [her] brain bred islands"—now was "true," since she was writing directly, openly, "confessionally" (and we knew her reservations about *that*) about her solitude, herself?

Not so fast: a corrective to my selective listening was on its way, just a heartbeat from the end:

Friday was nice. Friday was nice and we were friends. If only he had been a woman! I wanted to propagate my kind, and so did he, I think, poor boy. He'd pet the baby goats sometimes, and race with them, or carry one around. Pretty to watch; he had a pretty body.

Dangerous subject matter is how Merrill, in his memoir, explained Bishop's famous reticence, the way she "invented a familiar, 'harmless' situation" to dramatize "forbidden topics"— which suggests that the historical persona was deliberate camouflage, behind which to elegize her companion, Lota de Macedo Soares, or even to enact a retrospective on the shipwreck of her childhood. But since transparency defeats camouflage, another explanation may be O'Connor's, that "the imagination is not free, but bound." What is now most striking about "Crusoe in England" is not that it's a love poem ("One Art" is more explicit), or that it opens the door to autobiography (her prose piece "In the Village" goes further), but that it narrates, in parable, and as she never did in memoir or essays, her life as an artist. Through the figure of Crusoe, Bishop recasts her sandpiper with human longing still attached, making "a delicate adjustment of the outer and inner worlds in such a way that, without changing their nature, they can be seen through each other." By that light, Bishop's restraint and indirection seem a good deal like O'Connor's self-knowledge, less a ruse or a withholding, less a way to CONCEAL feelings, than a way to release and honor them.

There is no grandeur in Bishop, nothing Faulknerian or Yeatsian. For her Crusoe there is "no detail too small"—

I knew each nick and scratch by heart,
the bluish blade, the broken tip,
the lines of wood-grain on the handle . . .
the flute, the knife, the shriveled shoes,
my shedding goatskin trousers
(moths have got in the fur),
the parasol that took me such a time
remembering the way the ribs should go.

Such attention derives from a kind of humility, a "habit of being," the shore bird "watching his toes / —Watching, rather, the spaces of sand between them." And no romanticizing the profession, either, no portrait in oils:

> The world is a mist. And then the world is
> minute and vast and clear. The tide
> is higher or lower. He couldn't tell you which.
> ("Sandpiper")

> And I had waterspouts. Oh,
> half a dozen at a time, far out,
> they'd come and go, advancing and retreating,
> their heads in cloud, their feet in moving patches
> of scuffed-up white.
> Glass chimneys . . .
> . . . .
>   . . . I watched
> the water spiral up in them like smoke.
> Beautiful, yes, but not much company.
> ("Crusoe in England")

According to Louise Glück, "Poems *are* autobiography, but divested of the trappings of chronology and comment, the metronomic alternation of anecdote and response" (*Proofs and Theories*). Without chronology and comment, what is autobiography if not character? And on what other grounds should a hero, a model, make a claim on us? For me, the prized exemplars have been those who located "mystery and manners" on such unpromising ground as this:

> [O]ne tree snail, a bright violet-blue
> with a thin shell, crept over everything,
> over the one variety of tree,
> a sooty, scrub affair.
> Snail shells lay under these in drifts
> and, at a distance,

you'd swear that they were beds of irises.
There was one kind of berry, a dark red.

From an unassuming berry, Crusoe managed to concoct a
Dionysian portion, "the awful, fizzy, stinging stuff / that went
straight to my head." Like Bishop's poems, it was "Home-made,
home-made! But aren't we all?" So characteristically offhand,
that last line, and so crucial to the sensibility. The insight is taken
up and examined in another poem Bishop read that evening,
from *Geography III*:

> Suddenly, from inside,
> came an *oh!* of pain
> —Aunt Consuelo's voice—
> not very loud or long. . . .
> I might have been embarrassed,
> but wasn't. What took me
> completely by surprise
> was that it was *me*:
> my voice, in my mouth.
> Without thinking at all
> I was my foolish aunt,
> I—we—were falling, falling. . . .
>
> How—I didn't know any
> word for it—how "unlikely" . . .
> How had I come to be here,
> like them, and overhear
> a cry of pain that could have
> got loud and worse but hadn't?

Those lines are from a memorable poem about self and other, life
and art, called "In the Waiting Room," which sent me back to
reread O'Connor as a grown-up. Two "home-made" heroes, then,
with a lesson it took me years to recognize, a lesson I'm still trying to learn: that the "life" is inextricable from the work; for a
writer, they are the same thing.

Poetry and Gender

> As to the poetical Character itself, . . . it is not
> itself—it has no self—it is every thing and
> nothing—It has no character. . . . It is a wretched
> thing to confess; but is a very fact that not one word
> I ever utter can be taken for granted as an opinion
> growing out of my identical nature—how can it,
> when I have no nature?
>   —John Keats, letter to Richard Woodhouse

Although few poets may be left who fully endorse Keats's definition of "poetical character," surprisingly many, some of them women, do believe still that the individual self of the artist—sexual, ethnic, historical, political, and geographical—is subverted to the uses and priorities of his or her art. Few of those, however, will say so as bluntly as Elizabeth Bishop did: "Undoubtedly gender does play an important part in the making of any art, but art is art and to separate writings, paintings, musical compositions, etc., into two sexes is to emphasize values in them that are *not* art" (letter to Joan Keefe). Such a position, taken in the face of widespread efforts to replace "individual" with "collective" in defining the self, is not merely unfashionable but politically retrograde, for it is with the fervor of revolution that much has been written about "women's literature" in the past decade.

The bias against women in publication history, corresponding easily to the cultural bias Mary Ellmann discusses thoroughly, and wittily, in *Thinking about Women*, is well documented. In roughly eight hundred years of English literature, only the most recent one hundred have included substantial participation by women. In the past thirty years, however, that participation has increased astonishingly—a fine endorsement of free enterprise, so rapidly did publishers respond to the demands of women as a book-buying constituency—and contemporary writers who so wish are now able to find models of their own gender in great variety.

Clearly, anthologies and journals devoted exclusively to work by women, as well as feminist criticism and the women's political movement, were important factors in the reversal. But the establishment of a separate-but-equal category was accompanied by a broader claim: that this literary work belongs to a distinct, parallel tradition with its own purposes, criteria, and aesthetic priorities. Alicia Ostriker rebuts Bishop this way: "The belief that true poetry is genderless—which is a disguised form of believing that true poetry is masculine—means that we have not learned to see women poets generically, to recognize the tradition they belong to, or discuss either the limitations or strengths of that tradition" (*Stealing the Language*). This view has often been made imperative by the premise that women were excluded from the canon not only because of sexist bias among individual critics, reviewers, anthologists, prize-givers, and the like but because sexism has inhered within the very definitions of art, deposited there by its (primarily male) practitioners. Whether intended as adversarial or merely just, the us/them division long insured by *them*, and only briefly seen to diminish somewhat in bookstores and periodicals, was restored by *us*.

The complexity of this issue is compounded by the breadth of the label in general use, "women writers." The coinage appears direct and uncomplicated, but the use of a noun as a modifier is never without some ambiguity: does the term indicate women who write or writers who are women? That is, what is the relative importance of gender to an aesthetic? As Randall Jarrell pointed out, the pigs are seldom asked what they think about bacon. But has any other critical classification conscripted so many writers a priori?

In *Stealing the Language*, Ostriker dismissed such concern:

> [M]ost critics and professors of literature, including modern literature, deny that "women's poetry," as distinct from poetry by individual women, exists. Some women writers agree. Some will not permit their work to appear in women's anthologies. . . . Yet we do not hesitate to use the term "American poetry" (or "French poetry" or "Russian poetry") on the grounds that American (or French or Russian) poets are diverse. Should we call Whitman, Frost, and Stevens "poets" but not "American poets"?

At issue, of course, is the extent to which the label is meant to describe the work. Both Walt Whitman and Robert Frost were self-consciously "American," which is to say they saw such an affiliation as primary to their projects and strove to make poems from a local (rather than British) idiom. Thus, we can locate in their work characteristics that correspond to what we think of as "American poetry," later revised and refined by William Carlos Williams and others, particularly in regard to style and diction. With Wallace Stevens, the case is far more difficult, and the term runs the risk of obscuring both his intentions and his achievement. With Stevens, we use the label for convenience—something like putting the duckbill platypus in with the mammals—and for the illumination of contrast, and for the chance to claim him.

Even so, the influence of Ralph Waldo Emerson, say, can be traced in Stevens, whereas a parallel importance of Anne Bradstreet to Bishop or to Sylvia Plath is harder to track. Ostriker invited the equation: "In what follows I therefore make the assumption that 'women's poetry' exists in much the same sense that 'American poetry' exists. It has a history. It has a terrain. Many of its practitioners believe it has something like a language." But she avoided the direct question of *literary* precursors, presenting virtually no evidence that women were heavily influenced by other women's work (as distinct from the example of their success) prior to the 1960s; instead, the "history" presented was largely the story of how literary work by women has been received—which in turn reflected the way women have been viewed in the culture.

A similar sociological focus pervades Sandra Gilbert and Susan Gubar's *Norton Anthology of Literature by Women*. In the introductory material to each section the editors located individual women within the contours of the existing tradition, acknowledging that women "were influenced by" (and influenced) male writers, but they supplanted the usual literary periods with others that correspond to significant changes in the cultural attitudes toward and life patterns of women. The structure of the book, then, grouped writers according to similarities of the circumstance in which they wrote; similarities within the work itself were left to brief introductory comment, proximity, and the shaping influence of the editors' choices. That influence, of course, is pronounced: like Ostriker, though less insistent, the editors preferred instances of women writing directly about distinctly female, rather than universal human, experience. If the anthology is faulted on which writers, or which examples of their work, were thought representative, and faulted more vigorously than usual, it is because the category is so diverse and the lens so circumscribed: which animal, indeed, can represent the mammals?

Ostriker, on the other hand, took the similarity of circumstance to be equivalent to a similarity of aesthetic purpose and worked this assumption both vertically (Bradstreet to Judy Grahn) and horizontally (as in the curious pairing of Bishop and Anne Sexton). She said in her introduction that her subject was "the extraordinary tide of poetry by American women in our own time," an "increasing proportion" of which "is explicitly female in the sense that the writers have chosen to explore experiences central to their sex and to find forms and styles appropriate to their exploration." She used 1960 as an "approximate point of departure," listing "breakthrough and highly influential books" by poets whose publication dates coincided with the emerging women's political movement and the discovery of *The Second Sex* in this country (and the publication of Lowell's *Life Studies*). Some of these poets defined their aesthetic with gender primary in the definition; some located precursors among women of earlier generations. For Ostriker, the most influential figure among them was Adrienne Rich, who is listed with sixty-eight references in the index (as compared with ten for Mona Van Duyn and eleven for Muriel Rukeyser, two other "breakthrough poets"); at least, the feminist agenda articulated by Rich in the 1970s seemed to correspond to the "new thing" Ostriker applauded, which she allowed was "notoriously difficult to define precisely."

It may have been somewhat foggy in the minds of its pioneers as well, insofar as Rich, Rukeyser, Plath, Sexton, Denise Levertov, and others were working independently in the 1960s—not collectively, as the Transcendental or Black Mountain poets may be said to have been. Nevertheless, Ostriker undertook to locate the foundation of this "tide" or renascence in earlier writers and depended on the consistent difficulty of the woman writer's position to make her case, introducing many of the women cited with a succinct career summary. In doing so, she added to Gilbert and Gubar's notion of "anxiety of literary authority" a close attention to various women's sense of audience and where it impinged on or enabled the poetry. In fact, the question of audience might have provided a stable thesis for the entire book; certainly it made germane her recurring reference to mistreatment and misreading by the critics—those poets who wish/wished to articulate an aesthetic of gender are the same group, essentially, as those who identified their readership, or constituency, as primarily women. In particular, in discussions of Emily Dickinson's "duplicity" and the hard ("exoskeletal") style of many contemporary women, both viewed as responses to audience, the book comes closest to pointing out the kind of aesthetic similarities that might suggest literary affinity. But whereas with Bradstreet and Dickinson, who offer historically isolated oeuvres, Ostriker's book considers individual pieces both as poems and as sociopolitical documents, after that it seems impatient with such detail; her primary purpose—to describe an exclusive aesthetic through survey—led her to a focus on theme and a reliance on paraphrase that left transitions from the sociological to the literary largely unsupported.

One way to secure a connection among women writing in different periods and with differing aesthetic priorities would be to work deductively from a comprehensive theory of feminine psychology. Ostriker presented no such theory on which to base her arguments and, in fact, overtly resisted the method ("I attempt to read by the light that poems themselves emit, rather than by the fixed beam of one or another theory"). Nevertheless, many of her generalizations, in their easy exchange of "woman" and "woman poet," imply that primary similarities exist within the psychology of all women and inexorably shape the literature women make, regardless of the conscious intentions of the makers.

Even as a rigorous and comprehensive theory of feminine psychology has begun to emerge, the literary question continues to be muddied to the extent that poetry always confounds psychology: that is, the disciplines of art often transform or override the imperatives of the individuated ego. What continues to fascinate is what Ostriker's introduction promises to explore: the question of style—that is, the arrangement of aesthetic elements independent of subject matter. *Stealing the Language* chastises those reviewers and critics who condemned work because of its "feminine style" (for example, the elegance of Louise Bogan) even while it supports their basic premise—that style is identifiable as to gender—in Ostriker's own practice (for example, the self-effacement of Bradstreet). Yet her stylistic examples almost always double as examples of theme or subject.

Ellmann's discussion of tone in *Thinking about Women* is to the point here. After analyzing prose passages that demonstrate in their diction and syntax the authoritative tone, Ellmann located its rise (and its association with the masculine) in the nineteenth century, noting that earlier no distinction had been fixed between the intellectual authority and intimate emotion in Donne's sermons:

> But such a distinction is endemic to the nineteenth century. It was then, when women first began to publish not only as novelists but as (what we call) intellectuals, that a method of male utterance codified itself; and, as a result, a genuine difference seemed discernible between the ways in which men think and write, and the ways in which women think and write. . . . So Dickens recorded his conviction that George Eliot's *Scenes from Clerical Life*, published anonymously, must be written by a woman. The dichotomy was established: the dominant and masculine mode possessing the properties of reason and knowledge, the subsidiary and feminine mode possessing feelings and intuitions. If this dichotomy was unreal, it was not less dedicated on the part, particularly, of the dominant mode.

That Ellmann did find it "unreal"—though she included instances of women and men in this century perpetuating the dichotomy—is made definite in her disagreement with Virginia Woolf. Here is her quotation from Woolf:

> [Dorothy Richardson] has invented, or, if she has not invented, developed and applied to her own uses, a sentence which we might call the psychological sentence of the feminine gender. It is of a more elastic fibre than the old, capable of stretching to the extreme, of suspending the frailest particles, of enveloping the vaguest shapes. Other writers of the opposite sex have used sentences of this description and stretched them to the extreme. But there is a difference. Miss

Richardson has fashioned her sentence consciously, in order that it may descend to the depths and investigate the crannies of Miriam Henderson's consciousness. It is a woman's sentence, but only in the sense that it is used to describe a woman's mind by a writer who is neither proud nor afraid of anything that she may discover in the psychology of her sex.

Then Ellmann's crisp reply:

But, in fact, it seems impossible to determine a sexual sentence. As Virginia Woolf herself makes clear, the only certain femininity is in Dorothy Richardson's subject. Her sentence has more in common with Henry James' or Joyce's than with, say, George Eliot's.

And a sentence of Richardson's promptly follows as evidence.

What Ellmann contrasted to the "now outmoded" tone of authority was the use of wit, defined as the "means of relinquishing authority." Ostriker made a similar point but claimed the tactic as feminine; Ellmann, acknowledging that she had "perhaps not helped at all those obsessed readers like Dickens who are bent upon identifying the sex of writers," summarized this way: "As both simple authority and simple sensibility have become anachronistic, writers cohabit an area of prose in which sudden alternations of the reckless and the sly, the wildly voluble and the laconic, define only a mutual and refreshing disturbance of mind." That observation appeared in 1968, when Ostriker's "*quelque chose* DE NOUVEAU" was underway, and prefigures this passage from Carol Gilligan's *In a Different Voice* (1982), a study of psychological theory and women's development:

The different voice I describe is characterized not by gender but theme. Its association with women is an empirical observation, and it is primarily through women's voices that I trace its development. But this association is not absolute, and the contrasts between male and female voices are presented here to highlight a distinction between two modes of thought and to focus a problem of interpretation rather than to represent a generalization about either sex. In tracing development, I point to the interplay of these voices within each sex and suggest that their convergence marks times of crisis and change.

There is not much interest in "interplay" in *Stealing the Language*. The book is structured chronologically with a specific look at Bradstreet and Dickinson, then an examination of later poems paired by theme, and finally a catalogue of proliferating examples. Although the method is inductive, however, the mind-set is deductive: that is, Ostriker left as assumptions—and read by their light—the notions that gender is pronounced in poems and that a tradition of women's work exists and can be described. In addition, her preference for contemporary gender-specific poetry undermined her scholarship: the characteristics of individual poets' work are analyzed at the outset, when examples are few, but summarized and asserted at the very point of diversity where support for the argument is crucial. And finally there is the overriding oxymoronic wish, embodied in the label "women's poetry," simultaneously for the inclusive (all women) and for the exclusive (no men), whereby TRADITION rather than MOVEMENT might become a legitimate designation.

Impatience is often attendant on conviction. Since Ostriker was redressing imbalance and said she was confined to only a fraction of the poems she "would have enjoyed discussing," perhaps she assumed that the established Other would speak of itself/himself in the margins of her pages. But some comparison of Bradstreet with Edward Taylor's self-effacing, domestic imagery ("Make me, O Lord, Thy spinning wheel complete") is necessary to establish those qualities as unmistakably female. Likewise, the discussion of Plath's "feminine" treatment of the divided self is unconvincing without any mention of the idea of the double which already existed in literature (and was the subject of Plath's honors essay at Smith). Elizabeth Bishop's "In the Waiting

Room" is clearly a great poem, but did Ostriker mean to suggest that "the quest for identity" occurs more in Bishop than in Lowell? that contemporary women who "reverse man's division from nature" do not read Gerard Manley Hopkins or Theodore Roethke or Walt Whitman? This is to say not that Ostriker failed entirely to make direct comparisons with male writers but that material was too often chosen strictly to illuminate difference. If women writers are more playful than men, it should be demonstrated in light of John Berryman, Kenneth Patchen, or John Ashbery; if Plath's view of death as perfection in *Ariel* differs from that in the earlier "Sailing to Byzantium," the case needs to be made.

Ostriker might address these reservations with numbers— might reply that more women share Yeats's and Plath's vision than do men, that the characteristics she enumerated occur repeatedly in the work of contemporary women but only rarely in the work of men. She suggested as much in her general method, in her reliance (in the book's second half) on paraphrase and commentary rather than analysis of the poems, and in such considerations of style as do occur. To borrow a sentence from Ellmann, however, "Quantity here [about the topic of femininity], as elsewhere, suggests the strength of the proleptic impulse: the desire to prove is abundant even when proof is not." Consider the quantification, for instance, behind Ostriker's statement that "whether or not they deal directly with the self, or with sexuality as such, contemporary women poets employ anatomical imagery both more frequently and far more intimately than male poets." The footnote reveals that Ostriker's samples of one thousand lines each by male and female poets, on which she predicated the claim, were taken from, on the one hand, general anthologies of 1962 and 1969 (Stephen Berg and Robert Mezey's *Naked Poetry*, and Donald Hall's *Contemporary Poetry*) and, on the other, *Rising Tides*, a 1973 anthology dedicated to the presentation of an alternative, distinctly female, and previously neglected poetry: that is, a collection in which reference to the female self, thereby the body, was surely one criterion for inclusion.

At the end of the footnote, Ostriker added the following comment: "A different selection might of course have produced slightly different figures, but if the selection were made from poems published only in the 1970s, the gap between masculine reticence and feminine expressiveness about the body would appear even more pronounced." Struck by such adamant speculation, I tried my own limited test. To avoid perpetuating the editorial preference unavoidable in anthologies, I went directly to the poets and chose from my shelf the first three books by women, then the first three by men, which were published in the 1970s, contained at least fifty pages (I surveyed only the first fifty), and relied typically on a poetic line of roughly five to eight syllables (like Ostriker, I was too lazy to count words). Here are my findings, ordered by preponderance of references to the body, both parts and functions (sweating, bleeding, giving birth, having sex, and so on):

204   Galway Kinnell, *The Book of Nightmares* (1971)
162   Philip Levine, *The Names of the Lost* (1976)
118   Robert Hass, *Field Guide* (1973)
110   Tess Gallagher, *Instructions to the Double* (1976)
 67   Sandra McPherson, *The Year of Our Birth* (1978)
 40   Elizabeth Bishop, *Geography III* (1976)

Of course, books published in the 1970s could have collected work initially published earlier. Perhaps, too, limiting review to the first fifty pages skewed the data: if anatomical reference is a bold and subversive act, one might well save it for the back of the book. So I extended my research to six more poets, whose most recent books were stacked on my desk, this time disregarding line length and surveying all the pages of each book. Here are the additional findings, ranked according to average number of body references per page:

4.2   Stephen Dobyns, *Black Dog, Red Dog* (1984)
2.6   Gregory Orr, *We Must Make a Kingdom of It* (1986)
2.3   Lisel Mueller, *Second Language* (1986)

1.9   Thomas Lux, *Half-Promised Land* (1986)
1.5   Heather McHugh, *A World of Difference* (1981)
1.3   Mary Oliver, *Dream Work* (1986)

As for the qualitative difference claimed by Ostriker: Mueller (highest average among the women) used twenty-one references to eyes (including eyeholes and eyelashes), sixteen to head and face, ten to arms, twenty to hands, and twelve to skin; specific mention is made of fingernails, wrist, and temples, but mainly there are asexual teeth, bones, blood, heart, and "body." The list does not differ significantly in Lux, most anatomically reticent among the men—skin, hair, fingers, and head recur—except for his single-usage nouns: synapse, cranium, breasts, calf, jaw, rib, chin, ankles, skull, groin, heartbone, elbow, liver; spine appears twice, spit twice, lungs three times; there is no mention of voice (six times in Mueller).

My study is as statistically insignificant, and inconclusive, as Ostriker's, suggesting mainly that we were not reading the same poets—but Ostriker claimed to describe my library as well as hers. Meanwhile, her zeal for keeping men out is matched by her eagerness to bring women in under the categorical umbrellas. And though I should be glad to have an expanded reading list, she breezed past the actual poems so quickly that no evidence arose for replacing Mary Oliver with Sharon Barba or Yosana Akiko as representative of women's attitudes toward nature; for the first of these alternatives there is only one sample of nature imagery— "that dark watery place"—and for the second, no quotation at all. The handling of familiar poems too relies predominantly on paraphrase and on unfamiliar readings that go unsupported. There is only this about Louise Glück's "Portrait," which Ostriker cites as an example of "women's invisibility poems" in which "there is usually a sexual script" and "the poet is perhaps erotically dependent": "Louise Glück, a poet fascinated with border states between existence and nonexistence, in 'Portrait' imagines herself a child drawing a figure that is only an outline, 'white all through,' until *a lover* draws the heart [my italics]."

Now the full text (not provided by Ostriker) of the poem thus paraphrased:

Portrait

A child draws the outline of a body.
She draws what she can, but it is white all through,
she cannot fill in what she knows is there.
Within the unsupported line, she knows
that life is missing; she has cut
one background from another. Like a child,
she turns to her mother.
And you draw the heart
against the emptiness she has created.

Why Ostriker ignored the established scene and immediate referent (mother), in reading the penultimate pronoun (you) and direct address, is not revealed.

Hurrying to establish category and similarity, a common "terrain," Ostriker, herself a poet, too often failed to note difference, to bother with tone and nuance, with complexity—and what is poetry without these? Notably absent also in her book is discrimination. Sexton's small lyric "Housewife" is simply not of sufficient heft to balance "at an opposite pole" Bishop's "In the Waiting Room," yet the two poems receive equal treatment as examples of the quest for identity. Finally, "women writing strongly as women" are not always writing strongly as poets. Ostriker's book summarizes far more than it quotes, and when it does quote, the lines are often so flat, so devoid of interesting syntax, imagery, word choice, and rhythm as to make one wonder on what grounds, beyond thematic example, they are commended to the reader. Since the quotations are usually brief, it seems unfair to repeat them here, but surely Eloise Healy would not wish to be represented only by these lines:

Your god wears a mosaic suit
of hard mirrors and his clothes are too small.

They pinch him like metaphysics. . . .
He has never perspired, has no handkerchief.
He is barely aware you worship him,
fretting as he does about his own existence.

When *The Norton Anthology of Literature by Women* first appeared, a substantial amount of venom was exchanged in letters to the editor after Gail Godwin's negative but mild review in the *New York Times*. Part of the passion derived from the historical moment: given the long siege, the tacticians must have expected disagreements in the trenches to be set aside for a solid front against the enemy. (Perhaps this is why Ostriker chose to treat the "strengths" of women's poetry and not the "limitations.")

But the divergence of opinion among women about what makes good art is at least as vigorous of that of the literary population at large, and it is naturally manifested when books such as *The Norton Anthology of Literature by Women* or *Stealing the Language* appear, books that purport to describe the field but have in mind a particular battalion. Similar outbreaks attended the Berg and Mezey anthology mentioned earlier, *Naked Poetry*, as they will always greet examples of the time-honored tactic—asserting a minority position as the true and unsung majority view or the wave of the future. As with the Beat movement, conviction has intensified around the question of "women's literature" because it engages the nonliterary community as well: poems, which are also social documents, can provide confirmation of the critique of culture going on elsewhere.

Another recognized tactic, which can sometimes rankle, is for the oppressed to confirm the very qualities charged against them and convert condemnation into praise. It is hard to review Ostriker's list of feminine characteristics—intimacy, eroticism, anger, the divided self, nature as an extension of the female body—without recalling the stereotypes she rightly decried ("virgin or whore, angel or vixen, love-object, temptress or muse"). The relegation of women to feelings and intuition, as opposed to reason and knowledge, remains vigorous in a passage such as this:

As with women's erotic fantasies, the sensation of release rather than control is an aesthetic effect sought by women poets of all stripes. . . . [T]he imperative of intimacy often seems to shift the center of gravity in women's poems to a center of levity. . . . They joke, they play, they are silly, they are ludicrous—which is to say they are *ludic*: anti-Apollonian, Dionysiac, Carnavalesque[;] . . . there surfaces in women's poems a kind of giddy glee. . . . We may compare [Kathleen] Fraser's dance metaphor ["boogaloo of joy"] with Yeats' ecstatic solemnity in the dance trope at the close of "Among School Children" or Eliot's liturgical tone describing the dance in "East Coker."

Compare that from Ostriker with this from Joseph Addison (quoted by Ellmann):

Women in their nature are much more gay and joyous than men; whether it be that their blood is more refined, their fibres more delicate, and their animal spirits more light; vivacity is the gift of women, gravity that of men.

One celebrates and the other patronizes, but what else has changed?

In *Stealing the Language*, Ostriker's anti-Apollonian, Dionysiac alignment for women is not made explicitly in connection with Bradstreet but appears soon thereafter. In the first chapter— which includes a review of the pressures exerted on American women to be modest and self-effacing—there is this conclusion:

These women [Reese, Guiney, Crapsey, Teasdale, Wylie, Millay, Taggard, Bogan] composed the first substantial body of lyric poetry which is worth anything in the United States . . . yet their collective impact is not acknowledged as a movement, nor has it had an impact on critical theory.

There are several reasons for this neglect, all perhaps subsumed in the observation that men, not women, have written most of the literary manifestos in the twentieth century. . . .

[M]odernism took another direction, away from beauty as such, song as such. The great male moderns concern themselves with the decline of western values, the death of God, man's alienation from nature. If there is any single thing in common among Eliot, Pound, Frost, Stevens, and Williams, it is that these giant figures labor under a sense of devastating loss, which is seen as historical and social, and their work is a wrestling to erect some other saving structure. The women, however, tend to write like pagans, as if the death of God (and His civilization, and His culture, and His myths) were no loss to them. Indeed, it may have been a relief. A corollary difference is that the women write personally, whereas the reigning doctrine of modernism became impersonality: Yeats' "all that is merely personal soon rots," or the "extinction of personality" called for by Eliot.

It is difficult to untangle the various strands of assertion here, but the identification of women with the Natural Life Force, with Beauty and Song, with a personal rather than cultural focus, and away from the central ideas of the century, is self-evident, as is the linking of "personal" writing to what Bogan (who, like H.D. and Marianne Moore, was about as "personal" and "anti-intellectual" as Eliot) called "the line of feeling." Even were her generalizations accurate, Ostriker has supported a reductive—and limiting—equation between gender and form; if in fact she was right—if women's natural literary gift *is* this narrow—then literary mastery can be achieved only by exception to the gender characteristics she has cited, since great poetry from Donne to Dickinson has always encompassed both emotional intensity and intellectual rigor. Again, however, Ostriker has buried the literary question in political rhetoric: were it not for the winds of fashion, and the (male) Modernist manifestos, one would see that Reese, Guiney, Crapsey, Teasdale, et al., produced a body of work as significant as that of not only E. A. Robinson or Robinson Jeffers, other poets swept out by the modernist broom, but Eliot, Pound, Frost, Stevens, and Williams as well.

At the Skidmore College Millay Conference in October 1986 — a celebration of the receipt of Millay's papers by the college — Modernism was also the primary villain, diverting attention from hard assessment. After Millay's biographer, Nancy Milford, provided an introduction to the figure; after the critics' panel recounted the sexist reviews and the reputation's decline (but quoted no actual lines by Millay); after Richard Eberhart, Katha Pollitt, and I read some of our own poems and Eberhart delivered a tribute (he recalled best the slinky gown Millay wore when he first heard her read), the two women on the poets' panel resurrected a question from the audience the night before: could it be that the talent was major but the work was not? that too much of it relied on a rigid and unauthentic persona, diction already archaic in the 1920s, and sentimentality? The author of *Zelda* had left early and could not comment, but the response of invited feminist critics was immediate: we had been blinded to Millay's virtues by Modernism. In fact, novelist Mary Gordon had suggested over dinner, perhaps our standards were themselves suspect. What was so bad about sentimentality? Was it not the established male tradition that had decided, in recoil from the quintessentially female, it should be eschewed?

One's answers—that it was not only Modernism that happened but modern life; that sentimentality is reductive and dangerous in its oversimplifications, whatever its source; that its source seems as easily male as female—are of course inadequate against the most persuasive tactic of all: discredit the victims' ability to recognize the extent to which they have been, to use the euphemism, *had*.

One practical virtue of anthologies is that they sometimes provide a larger, or different, taste of poets whose hash has been previously settled. Millay is represented in the standard *Norton Introduction to Literature* (fourth edition, 1986) only by two sonnets from 1923, "What lips my lips have kissed" and "I, being born a woman and distressed," also reprinted in the Norton-distributed *American Tradition in Literature* (vol. 2, fourth edition, Grosset & Dunlap, 1974). There is no entry at all in the revised edition of

The Norton Anthology of Poetry (1975); the third edition (1983) al-
lots two full pages—including the ubiquitous "I, being born a
woman," four entries from 1920 when Millay was twenty-eight,
and three pieces from the 1930s. *The Norton Anthology of Literature by Women* repeats the aphoristic "First Fig" and "Second
Fig," as well as the apparently irresistible "I, being born . . ." and
its contemporary "Oh, sleep forever in the Latmian cave," but
supplements that selection with free verse and idiomatic pieces
from the 1930s and 1950s as well as the full text of "Sonnets from
an Ungrafted Tree," a sequence that rivals but postdates Frost's
"Hill Wife" and "Home Burial" in its dramatic presentation of
character.

These newly included pieces were not, of course, the poems
that made her famous, and although it is salient to consider the
sexism that no doubt brightened the probing light cast on the
more facile and melodramatic poems, one should likewise not
forget that at midcareer, less than sixty years ago, Millay was writing lines such as

> Gone in good sooth you are: not even in dream
> You come. As if the strictures of the light,
> Laid on our glances to their disesteem,
> Extended even to shadows and the night;

and

> Ah, drink again
> This river that is the taker-away of pain,
> And the giver-back of beauty!

Such clunkers may yet prove interesting—one looks forward to
Milford's biography to suggest why this talent needed the confirmation of compatible manifestos when Dickinson's did not,
and whether feminine character is as susceptible as male to what
is tediously called the "bitch goddess" of success, and to what
extent Millay might be a more helpful model to young women
writing poems than Frost, another poet trapped in a persona.

Eventually, in-depth studies of individual writers may allow some insight into that entire group of "feminine sonneteers" (Bogan's phrase) writing early in the century; after all, the real issue is the relationship of poetry not to gender but to character, of which gender is merely one part.

The periodic Ezra Pound anniversaries, with their flurries of reassessment, remind us just how complicated that relationship is. As Ellmann noted, "[I]ndividual character is finally impenetrable, and the character, say, of an entire nation so obscure that to offer its definition is considered obscurantism, or worse. . . . But even those who despise the mode of thought cannot help but practice it. And a hope to repress sexual characterization, the most entrenched form of the general mode, would be . . . futile." "Gender-conditioning," a term in general use in women's studies, addresses character and straddles the old "nature versus nurture" debate. It suggests that although anatomy itself may no longer be destiny, the response to gender—expectations and strictures from the culture—is an equally determining force, imprinting the individual psyche as it develops. But even were this conditioning the same in every instance, surely the initial material was various, and poetry is at least as diverse as the population that produces it. When studying the poetry of a nation or a period, one must attend to the ways individual talents manifest different responses to similar circumstances. If female experience—whether deriving from some inherent feminine nature or in response to cultural bias—is to be the primary given, then one will better understand the poetry it informs by examining the *differences* between Bogan and Millay, Bishop and Sexton, Glück and Linda Pastan. If truly little difference is to be found, if contemporary women's poems do sound alike, treating the same themes with the same tone—as so many critical studies and so many journals and anthologies devoted exclusively to women would have us believe—then we must be writing very poorly indeed.

In a revolutionary time, every action or action eschewed is a political act. Some believe that what's best for women or gay men or ethnic minorities is for members of these groups to write increasingly about themselves, write with anger and polemic, disregarding what chafes and restrains. But as Tom McGrath explained in 1982:

> There have been a lot of tactical poems directed to particular things, and those poems now are good in a certain sort of way, but the events they were about *have moved out from under them* [original italics]. Somebody asked Engels, "What happened to all the revolutionary poetry of 1848?" He replied: "It died with the political prejudices of the time." ("The Frontiers of Language")

To believe that sexism or homophobia or racism are doomed prejudices may take greater idealism than one can muster, but what is best for poetry, including the poetry made by women, is fidelity to the most rigorous standards possible.

A young poet in Ames, Iowa, once confided to me that *The Norton Anthology of Literature by Women, No More Masks, Rising Tides,* and other anthologies of women's work had given her— a participant in writing classes taught primarily by men—permission to write about her own life, from a feminine sensibility. The footnote I make to her gratitude suggests an additional set of permissions: to write about something else if she chooses, to embrace Bishop or Berryman, Donne or Dickinson as legitimate precursors, or to differ from all who've come before as far as discipline, courage, and talent will support.

Rethinking Adjectives

In comparisons to John Donne in his 1921 essay on the Metaphysical poets, T. S. Eliot said, "Tennyson and Browning are poets, and they think; but they do not feel their thought as immediately as the odour of a rose." Set beside the sample he ferrets out of Tennyson, the assessment seems generous:

> One walked between his wife and child,
> With measured footfall firm and mild,
> And now and then he gravely smiled.
>> The prudent partner of his blood
>> Leaned on him, faithful, gentle, good,
>> Wearing the rose of womanhood.
>> And in their double love secure,
>> The little maiden walked demure,
>> Pacing with downward eyelids pure.
>> These three made unity so sweet,
>> My frozen heart began to beat,
>> Remembering its ancient heat.

Eliot certainly knew how to play to the jury. Because the occasion, the "conflict" (such as it is), and the characters (types, actually) are wholly expected, the poem seems to have little purpose *except* embellishment: that is, modification substitutes for thought. Almost every noun has its attached sanction, and the most pious (*footfall, partner, maiden, eyelids, unity*) have two or three or four, all cousins in virtue. Six of these are placed in positions of high attention—in the rhyme scheme—with syntax inverted twice to do so. The verse, then, falls to platitude: *measured, firm, mild, grave* husband; *prudent, faithful, gentle, good* wife; the child *in their double love secure, demure,* and *pure* of eyelid. Who wouldn't prefer, with Yeats, a poetry "as cold and passionate as the dawn"?

Of course, ornament had been around for centuries before Tennyson; bad poets and good had found it handy for padding out a metered line, for inflating the subject matter, for convincing the reader of the poet's earnestness or sensitivity. But the Modernists challenged more than abuse. A part of speech with little syntactical necessity, an "adjective"—from the root meaning "to annex"—is "an addition or adjunct; that which is added to or dependent on a substantive as an attribute." A tough, hard, sinuous poetry, an economical poetry, a poetry autonomous from its maker, would precipitate a bias: for nouns and verbs left unadorned.

As Ernest Hemingway demonstrated to the point of parody, the noun is the strongest part of speech. Without nouns there is no poem—perhaps, one might venture, there is no language: if language points to, or names, then the *nomen* is language at its most functional. In a poem, nouns embody—concrete nouns, the substance of the world; abstract nouns, the substance of the mind— and give the poem weight, density, and significance. The power of naming confirms the world: with *Mama, cup, water, doggie, moon,* every new Adam comes into speech and into the world beyond the self. Pound supplied the argument in his distinction between the lyric and rhetoric, on the one hand, and a poetry of images on the other:

> There is a sort of poetry where music, sheer melody, seems as if it were "just coming over into speech."
>
> There is another sort of poetry where painting or sculpture seems as if it were "just coming over into speech."

The first sort of poetry has long been called "lyric." . . .

The other sort of poetry is as old as the lyric and as honorable, but, until recently, no one had named it. Ibycus and Liu Ch'e presented the "image." Dante is a great poet by reason of this faculty, and Milton is a wind-bag because of his lack of it. The "image" is the furthest possible remove from rhetoric. Rhetoric is the art of dressing up some unimportant matter so as to fool the audience for the time being. So much for the general category. Even Aristotle distinguishes between rhetoric, "which is persuasion," and the analytical examination of truth. ("Vorticism")

An aesthetic, then, of nouns. First, because the noun is the source of the image—a verb needs an agent, someone or something that runs, sings, talks. Second, because an "analytical examination of truth," striving to collapse the distance between language and the external world, fosters suspicion of annexed qualities, which may distort, obscure, or contaminate. Even for description and comparison, the noun, by virtue of its syntactical power, would do the job better, one fact of the world juxtaposed against another, revealing empirical correspondences—

Like a fly upon a stream
His mind moves upon silence.

By extension, if convincing emotional response needs to be another such fact it is also best relegated to nouns:

The only way of expressing emotion in the form of art is by finding an "objective correlative"; in other words, a set of objects, a situation, a chain of events which shall be the formula of that *particular* emotion; such that when the external facts, which must terminate in sensory experience, are given, the emotion is immediately evoked. (Eliot, "Hamlet and His Problems," in *The Sacred Wood*)

Of course, if a poem were nothing but nouns, there would be little subordination and emphasis—a pale imitation indeed of painting or sculpture. What carries the poem over "into speech" is syntax; and syntax, parts of speech in relation to one another, is accomplished by the predicate. If the noun is fact, then the verb is movement, change, mutability. In the choice of a verb, the poet selects from the possible relationships among separate nouns and further directs with parallel or subordinate verb action:

> What but design of darkness to appal?
> If design govern in a thing so small.

Design, when attached to malevolence, is a horrible thing; *appal* prolongs horror (and duplicates, in the respondent, the very colorlessness of Frost's flower and spider) as an active and continuing force, while *govern*, by suggesting power, shifts the focus from response to cause.

Increased attention in the twentieth century to the organic movement of poems outside fixed forms, and to the poem as a "field of energy," increased the importance of the verb. Still, verbs are not crucial to the extent nouns are, as Robert Hass demonstrates in his influential poem "Meditation at Lagunitas." Its thirty-one lines contain only eleven independent predicates, and these are neutral, languid: *is, resembles, we talked, there was, I understood, there was, I remembered, it hardly had to do with her, I must have been, I remember, there are.* Trailing these, the substance of the meditation is rendered in dependent clauses, as though simply received or recorded by the poet. Even at closure, the final lines are a sentence fragment, and the reach for resonance and enlargement rests on the placement of nouns—abstract, concrete, and repeated:

> Such tenderness, those afternoons and evenings,
> saying *blackberry, blackberry, blackberry.*

If predicates are this dispensable, how much more so adjectives! After all, "tender" is more amorphous than *tenderness,* "thirsty" less commanding than *thirst, wonder* more solemn and convincing than "wonderful," *despair* a good deal more respectable than "desperate." The debasement of adjectives is more widespread now than at the turn of the century, their descriptive prowess weakened by the direct image of photography, film, and television, their value judgments grown suspect in the wake of advertising's unsupported claims. Anything, it would seem, can be GREAT! WONDERFUL! SPLENDID! if we say it is, whereas most people probably still wish to believe that "greatness," "wonder" and "splendor" have some objective standards, some specific denotations, even if we can't agree on what they are. Abstracted "happiness" and "sadness" provide a veneer of shared condition, but "happy" belongs to me, as does "sad," and descriptive terms —short, tall, fat, thin, ugly, beautiful—are, we have learned, notoriously relative.

In the practice of craft, then, so heavily influenced by the Modernists' aesthetic revolution and their quarrel with late Victorian and Georgian poetry, adjectives became the rhetorical residue that set off the Geiger counter, particularly at moments like this one, when the poem makes its strongest claims:

> I lean back, as the evening darkens and comes on.
> A chicken hawk floats over, looking for home.
> I have wasted my life.
>> ("Lying in a Hammock on William Duffy's Farm
>> in Pine Island, Minnesota")

Although James Wright has risked, earlier, a few descriptive strokes for the "factual" surroundings (bronze butterfly, black trunk of the green tree, green shadow, empty house, golden stones), he shrewdly moves the poem to its enlargement with relaxed, suggestive, idiomatic verbs and blunt declarative statement, learned from Rilke, for the clincher: *I have wasted my life.* The direct exposition disarms us, balances the poem's ennui, its deeply Romantic premise. The tactic is clear enough: legitimize adjectival (that is, subjective, unsupported) impulses by converting them into more substantial parts of speech, as in these swatches from Sylvia Plath:

> Stasis in darkness
> Pour of tor and distances
>
> Pivot of heels and knees!—The furrow
> Splits and passes
>
> Something
> Hauls me through air—
> Thighs, hair;
> Flakes from my heels.
>
> And now I
> Foam to wheat, a glitter of seas.
> The child's cry
> Melts in the wall
> And I
> Am the arrow

A poetry kit, therefore, from which to make poems—the potent word in Eliot's configuration is "formula"—would include a long list of nouns, plenty of prepositions (to increase the opportunities for nouns), and optional vivid verbs. One need not even strain under complex syntax, since a great deal of nuance may be added through lacunae, fragmentation, juxtaposition. Following the New Criticism, which sheared from the text "extraneous" information about the poet, about the sensibility and intention that wrote the poem—following too the growth of the workshop and a methodology for teaching writing—there has emerged an impressive sophistication about how poems are made to work, how they are crafted. Technology can upgrade competence. And because technology thrives on rules, rules have grown in stringency. Not shy of dicta, Pound provided the motto: "Use no superfluous word, no adjective, which does not reveal something," and "use either no ornament or good ornament." Our further abridgment: beware the adjective altogether, since who dares claim a "good one" anymore?

The Modernists' antagonism toward the Romantics is not our quarrel. Increased scrutiny of their overcorrection seems long overdue, especially in light of new hesitation about the wholesale exclusion of rhetoric. My focus here is myopic, a reconsideration of such luminous and memorable effects as these:

What did I know, what did I know
of love's austere and lonely offices?
*
And we are here as on a darkling plain
Swept with confused alarms of struggle and flight,
Where ignorant armies clash by night.
*
The uncontrollable mystery on the bestial floor.
*
An aged man is but a paltry thing,
A tattered coat upon a stick
*
To be quiet in the fern
Like a thing gone dead and still,
Listening to the prisoned cricket
Shake its terrible, dissembling
Music in the granite hill.
*
. . . bird shapes—
Moving, elusive as fish, fearless,
Hanging, bunched like young fruit, bending the end
    branches,
Still for a moment,
Then pitching away in half-flight,
Lighter than finches.
*
Like a long-legged fly upon a stream
His mind moves upon silence.

Rather than adornment, or embellishment, the modifiers in these instances seem the very heart of the matter at hand—as do this final adverb and adjective, on which the shrewd verbs depend for the couplet's reverberating irony:

> What but design of darkness to appal?
> If design govern in a thing so small.

One might examine that sonnet for its effective adjectives throughout—except that it is, in truth, atypical: Frost usually builds poems with verbs of action and narrative, creating an apparently disinterested record; meanwhile, by eschewing adjectives he divests himself of the responsibility of opinion. But the text of "Ariel"—quoted earlier in fragments, modification suppressed—shows the opposite case:

> Stasis in darkness.
> Then the substanceless blue
> Pour of tor and distances.
>
> God's lioness,
> How one we grow,
> Pivot of heels and knees!—The furrow
>
> Splits and passes, sister to
> The brown arc
> Of the neck I cannot catch,
>
> Nigger-eye
> Berries cast dark
> Hooks—
>
> Black sweet blood mouthfuls,
> Shadows.
> Something else
>
> Hauls me through air—
> Thighs, hair;
> Flakes from my heels.

White
Godiva, I unpeel—
Dead hands, dead stringencies.

And now I
Foam to wheat, a glitter of seas.
The child's cry

Melts in the wall.
And I
Am the arrow,

The dew that flies
Suicidal, at one with the drive
Into the red

Eye, the cauldron of morning.

The adjectives are central, unapologetic, even shocking (my spell checker honorably refuses to recognize *nigger-eye*), often emphasized by hard enjambment. The use of color particularly contributes to the unity and movement of the poem, and to the audacity of the speaker—from the *substanceless blue / pour* at the opening; through the sensual shadows of *brown arc, dark hooks,* and *black sweet blood mouthfuls*; to the stanzaic yoking of *white* and *dead,* she makes ready for, and makes compelling, violent transcendence into the *red eye.* The placement of the adjectives at important structural moments establishes the tone, shapes the poem's meaning, and secures, in *suicidal,* our understanding of the dramatic verbs throughout.

Pound, Eliot, and others were correct in linking ornament to the subjective: it is precisely their location IN the subjective that makes adjectives indispensable to Plath's lyric, just as the meditative or discursive poem needs its nouns to chew on, the narrative its verbs to convey events in time and their consequences. A bad poem is easily recognized by excessive unsupported or stale adjectives; they most quickly reveal sloppiness or inauthenticity in the felt life of the poem. On the other hand, despite their syntactical weakness, or because of it, William Carlos Williams lets adjectives carry the crucial information in the following lyric, thereby forcing subjective, sensory response into significance, insisting that it is what is, and what matters:

This Is Just to Say

I have eaten
the plums
that were in
the icebox

And which
you were probably
saving
for breakfast

Forgive me
they were delicious
so sweet
and so cold

Without that last sentence, there is no poem. In a brilliant arrogance, the final assertions—*delicious / so sweet / and so cold*—both justify and undercut *Forgive me*. Pleasure first, virtue second, oh surely you understand.

"To modify" means to change or alter. Syntactically, the adjective provides enormous advantages of economy, since its family includes articles, comparatives, and participles. In participles the phrase or clause is collapsed into a single word—"music which dissembles" becomes "dissembling music"—thereby placing the subordinate verb in the most immediate conjunction possible to the noun and multiplying the number of verbs possible in an economical or compressed text. Comparison—"Ghostlier demarcation, keener sounds"—allows subtle discrimination and correspondence, and articles prevent a concrete noun (apple, tree, hand) from blurring into weightless generalization, rooting it instead in experience (an apple, the tree, a hand).

Both basic types of adjectives, then, the descriptive and the limiting, serve precision. "Fly" is a broad category of insect, and a housefly on water would be helpless and clumsy; it is *long-legged* that makes Yeats's simile accurate and insightful:

> Like a long-legged fly upon a stream
> His mind moves upon silence.

Likewise,

> An aged man is but a paltry thing,
> A tattered coat upon a stick

says something entirely different in actual denotation from

> A man is a thing,
> A coat upon a stick

or, to strip the lines of ALL adjectival syntax,

> Man is thing.

Adjectives can correct, contradict, or amplify the possible meanings within the noun.

Consider this list of adjectives from a modern poem: *round, slovenly, wild, tall, gray, bare*. If ever a list of words could seem unpromising, this would be it. On the other hand, the nouns in this poem are authoritative, identifiable, and repeated: *jar, Tennessee, hill, wilderness, hill, wilderness, jar, ground, port, air, dominion, jar, bird, bush, nothing, Tennessee*. A poem made viable by nouns of increasing abstraction? But it is, in fact, the adjectives that provide the argument of Wallace Stevens's poem. Without them, there is a series of unconvincing actions:

> I placed a jar in Tennessee
> upon a hill.

> It made the wilderness
> surround the hill.
> The wilderness rose up to it,
> and sprawled around.
> The jar was of a port in air.
> It took dominion everywhere.
> It did not give of bird or bush,
> Like nothing in Tennessee.

Who says so? Why? So what? The statements are not compelled unless the wilderness is *slovenly* and the jar *round, bare, gray*; the otherness of the artifact supplies its power, its dominion, but to name "otherness" is to abstract the action and cancel the essential nature of each. With adjectives, the wilderness can still sprawl although *no longer wild*, and the jar can remain small and unassuming even as it commands, a stroke of gray in a dense green painting. What's altered, or modified, are our assumptions about power:

Anecdote of the Jar

> I placed a jar in Tennessee,
> And round it was, upon a hill.
> It made the slovenly wilderness
> Surround that hill.
>
> The wilderness rose up to it,
> And sprawled around, no longer wild.
> The jar was round upon the ground
> And tall and of a port in air.
>
> It took dominion everywhere.
> The jar was gray and bare.
> It did not give of bird or bush,
> Like nothing else in Tennessee.

Of course, the poet's strategy of restraint contributes as well: no dramatic verbs for those adjectives to compete with, unmodified (read unspecific) nouns exactly where he wants them, the repeated, accruing pronoun—a severe texture in which *slovenly* is overmatched by *round*, now enlarged by repetition (*ground, surround, around*).

Modifiers not only supply crucial nuance—meaning—but can structure the poem as well: that is, one can trace in them the poem's movement. This list alone identifies another poem:

> stanza 1: *sudden, great, beating, staggering, dark, caught, helpless;*
> stanza 2: *terrified vague, feathered, loosening, laid, white, strange;*
> stanza 3: *broken, burning, dead;*
> stanza 4: *caught up, mastered, brute, indifferent.*

It is Yeats's great sonnet "Leda and the Swan":

> A sudden blow: the great wings beating still
> Above the staggering girl, her thighs caressed
> By the dark webs, her nape caught in his bill,
> He holds her helpless breast upon his breast.
>
> How can those terrified vague fingers push
> The feathered glory from her loosening thighs?
> And how can body, laid in that white rush,
> But feel the strange heart beating where it lies?
>
> A shudder in the loins engenders there
> The broken wall, the burning roof and tower
> And Agamemnon dead.
>   Being so caught up,
> So mastered by the brute blood of the air,
> Did she put on his knowledge with his power
> Before the indifferent beak could let her drop?

The opening quatrain defines an action, a struggle—something powerful against something helpless. The sestet examines the consequences of the event—historical violence engendered by sexual violence—and reaffirms what is extraordinary in the occasion. Within that broad and fairly predictable examination of the sensational, descriptors modify the usual assumptions. An early draft of the poem opened this way:

> Now can the swooping godhead have his will
> Yet hovers, though her helpless thighs are pressed
> By the webbed toes; and that all-powerful bill
> Has suddenly bowed her face upon his breast.

In the finished poem modifiers have been replaced, not cut. Now Leda is given equal time in the stanza; the antagonists alternate consistently (*her nape, his bill; her breast, his breast*), with even-handed modification (*great wings, staggering girl; caressed thighs, dark webs; wings beating, her helpless breast*), while the obvious references to power (*swooping godhead, will, all-powerful bill, bowed her face*) have been reduced. Since the *godhead* is providing all the action, this balance was possible only through increased subordinate syntax and modification, affording the human a greater presence in the poem.

The second stanza centers even more directly on Leda's response to Zeus and makes crucial to the poem, in the adjectives, the question of her participation in the event. With *loosening thighs*, a possible ambiguity enters: the sestet's *shudder in the loins* may be Leda's orgasmic shudder, as well as Zeus's. *Being so caught up, so mastered* are participles that suggest both victimization and rapture and make a genuine, not rhetorical, question in the famous final couplet:

> Did she put on his knowledge with his power
> Before the indifferent beak could let her drop?

The dramatic situation alone (god rapes girl) would have us answer *no*. The modifiers have suggested *maybe*. The revision, and its adjectives, introduce greater complexity into the mythic occasion; the power balance has been altered while the central figures retain their inherent characteristics.

Another way to modify or alter nouns is to contradict them with descriptors, and one poet does this so consistently that the paradoxical, even oxymoronic pairings are a stylistic trademark:

a novel agony	*severer triumph*
homely anguish	*a piercing comfort*
awful leisure	*ethereal blow*
marauding hand	*sovereign anguish*
imperial affliction	*signal woe*
poignant luxury	*sordid excellence*
unobtrusive mass	*superior bush*
minor nation	*divine majority*
a perfect, paralyzing bliss	*delicious accident*

Underlining this repeating pattern is her thoroughly idiosyncratic syntax:

After great pain, a formal feeling comes—
The nerves sit ceremonious, like Tombs—

Within that syntax, sinuous or abrupt as she chose, the poem lives in its crucial adjectives—*great pain, a formal feeling, ceremonious nerves, the stiff heart, the feet mechanical, a quartz contentment*. Throughout the poem those pairs forge a patient, exacting definition.

Most frequently Dickinson used the adjective to uncover the disguised threat within apparently desirable abstractions: *severer triumph, a piercing comfort, a sordid excellence, a paralyzing bliss*. This is surely the most economical and powerful use of paradox in literature, as well as one of the most brilliant illustrations of doubt. Here is just one unmasking of the falsely attractive:

Success is counted sweetest
By those who ne'er succeed.
To comprehend a nectar
Requires sorest need.

> Not one of all the purple Host
> Who took the Flag today
> Can tell the definition
> So clear of Victory
>
> As he defeated—dying—
> On whose forbidden ear
> The distant strains of triumph
> Burst agonized and clear!

From its opening superlatives through its careful use (or omission) of articles, the poem alters the nouns to provoke a more discriminating understanding of *success*—that it most achieves its character when unattained—and to enact the nature of longing along the way.

Adjectives, then, restore the eye, and the "I," to the poem; they supply tone, the context without which nouns can be imprecise, incomplete, and misleading. Even Eliot, that harrower of the adjectival, knew it—listen to the combination of despair and protest conveyed in this passage:

> April is the cruelest month, breeding
> Lilacs out of the dead land, mixing
> Memory and desire, stirring
> Dull roots with spring rain.
> Winter kept us warm, covering
> Earth in forgetful snow, feeding
> A little life with dried tubers.

To remove the modification is to remove meaning and power:

> The month of April breeds lilacs out of the land,
> mixes memory and desire, and stirs roots with rain.
> Winter kept us, and covered earth in snow,
> and fed life with tubers.

No matter how Eliot "objectifies"—*One thinks*, he says—his adjectives maintain in his poems the sensibility that shaped them:

One thinks of all the hands
That are raising dingy shades
In a thousand furnished rooms.

The "objects, situation, event" in "Preludes," the "external facts,
which must terminate in sensory experience," are not any hands,
shades, rooms—are not just the nouns, the things of the world
shorn of what perceives them, interprets and responds:

His soul stretched tight across the skies
That fade behind a city block,
Or trampled by insistent feet
At four and five and six o'clock:
And short square fingers stuffing pipes,
And evening newspapers, and eyes
Assured of certain certainties,
The conscience of a blackened street
Impatient to assume the world.

I am moved by fancies that are curled
Around these images, and cling:
The notion of some infinitely gentle
Infinitely suffering thing.

In short, adjectives not only annex precision and clarity, for
more exact meaning, and add nuance and resonance, for evocation of emotion; in their amplifications of tone they acknowledge
the poet's subjective presence in the poem. In fact, the adjective
perhaps springs more directly than any other part of speech from
the lyric source. To say so acknowledges a muttered charge that
lyric poetry may be, to some extent, regressive: that whereas the
narrative is social and cements the social bond, lyric skimps
"what happened" and "why it happened" and even "this is what it
meant"—although all those things may be part of a lyric poem—
and focuses primarily on "what it felt like." But the impulse is
investigative before it is expressive. When a baby comes into

speech, he begins by talking to himself, exploring the sounds he can make, discovering the source of that sound in a way both sensuous and cognitive. Later, he notices how the sounds attract an adult response—that is communication, and that is also power, and the parallel in poetry is the maturation of craft. But many great lyric poems, poems about death, love, history, and art, poems that communicate and teach and heal, may arise from some version of an infant holding her foot and making miraculous sounds: that is, may emanate from a deep alienation, the first experience—and perhaps, paradoxically, the only truly universal experience—of the individual self. Adjectives moderate between nominal fixity (the world's facts) and mutability (change enacted on them); they strengthen the noun by adding response to fact, by limiting or expanding the noun, and by admitting into the poem the human sensibility that is apart from the world, thereby putting the yearning self in alignment with the world.

Yeats has said,

> When sound, and colour, and form are in a musical relation, a beautiful relation to one another, they become as it were one sound, one colour, one form, and evoke an emotion that is made out of their distinct evocations and yet is one emotion. The same relation exists between all portions of every work of art whether it be an epic or a song, and the more perfect it is, and the more various and numerous the elements that have flowed into its perfection, the more powerful will be the emotion, the power, the god it calls among us. . . . It is indeed only those things which seem useless or very feeble that have any power. (*Essays and Introductions*)

If music is both sound and feeling, then adjectives are a crucial source of music in our poems, meditative or narrative or lyric. This useless, feeble part of speech can "evoke an emotion that is made out of [the] distinct evocations" of separate nouns, and that introduces "various and numerous elements." Because of its subjective nature its presence in the poem is the hardest to earn;

craft does not put it there so much as vision, intuition, temperament, perhaps even character. It does not provide the energy that moves the poem; it does not reside in syntactical necessity; it derives its strength less from external reality and common meaning than from a singular sensibility. Adjectives can betray an insufficient eye or imprecision at the poem's heart, and a poem offering nothing but expected or facile adjectives will quickly become a wallow. The easiest thing to do with this troublesome part of speech is to cut it out of the text or convert it to a noun or noun phrase—that way, we make the piece better resemble the gestures of a strong poem, though we may also make it anonymous: such is the cost of efficient technology. Writing workshops do that kind of cutting because only the poet can replace a weak adjective with an effective one, a task beyond the technical. But a lyric in English without any adjectives at all may be fraudulent, or merely afraid.

The Poems of Our Climate

I

Clear water in a brilliant bowl,
Pink and white carnations. The light
In the room more like a snowy air,
Reflecting snow. A newly-fallen snow
At the end of winter when afternoons return.
Pink and white carnations—one desires
So much more than that. The day itself
Is simplified: a bowl of white,
Cold, a cold porcelain, low and round,
With nothing more than the carnations there.

II

Say even that this complete simplicity
Stripped one of all one's torments, concealed
The evilly compounded, vital I

And made it fresh in a world of white,
A world of clear water, brilliant-edged,
Still one would want more, one would need more,
More than a world of white and snowy scents.

III

There would still remain the never-resting mind,
So that one would want to escape, come back
To what had been so long composed.
The imperfect is our paradise.
Note that, in this bitterness, delight,
Since the imperfect is so hot in us,
Lies in flawed words and stubborn sounds.

(Wallace Stevens)

Image

There are two usual ways to praise the image. The first assumes that art is representational or "imitative," recording and embodying the shared reality we think of as the world. From this largely classical aesthetic position the image is valued as "a picture made out of words," "the sensuous element in poetry," and

> the reproduction in the mind of a sensation produced by a physical perception. . . . When Archibald Macleish says, in "Ars Poetica," that a poem should be "Dumb / As old medallions to the thumb," he not only means that the language of poetry should make important use of imagery, he also exemplifies what he means by expressing it in terms of imagery. . . . When, however, he says "A poem should not mean / But be," his meaning is the same but his language is not, for this statement is abstract rather than concrete and imagery-bearing, dealing as it does with an idea or concept rather than a perception or sensation. (*Princeton Encyclopedia of Poetry and Poetics*)

The opposition within this definition is important: the image is not abstraction, not idea or concept, even as the examples that follow range from the literal use of concrete nouns (what I will call narrative detail) to simile and metaphor.

That range is apparent in this passage, for instance, which begins in exposition and moves quickly into figure:

> About halfway between West Egg and New York the motor
> road hastily joins the railroad and runs beside it for a quarter
> of a mile, so as to shrink away from a certain desolate area of
> land. This is a valley of ashes—a fantastic farm where ashes
> grow like wheat into ridges and hills and grotesque gardens.
> (F. Scott Fitzgerald, *The Great Gatsby*)

Detail suggests empirical evidence; it makes the text plausible. A figure, by comparing an object or experience to something familiar, adds clarity; it makes the text accessible. When poetry aspires to mirror the world, the image is valued for its representational power—its ability to suggest to the reader a color, say, which is an "ostensible copy or replica of the objective color itself" (*Princeton Encyclopedia*), or a sterile urban landscape, backdrop for duplicity and betrayal. Definitions acknowledge all five senses, but the primary sense in this aesthetic is sight, and the sister art to poetry is painting.

The second usual way to praise the image presumes a different project. M. H. Abrams uses the lamp, contrasted with the mirror, as his figure for "expressive theories" of art brought into play by the Romantic movement, whereby

> the conceptions burst out into a turbid stream, expressive
> in a manner of the internal conflict. . . . In a word, reason
> speaks literally, the passions poetically. *The mind, with what-*
> *ever passion it be agitated, remains fixed upon the object that*
> *excited it; and while it is earnest to display it, is not satisfied*
> *with a plain and exact description,* but adopts one agreeable
> to its own sensations, splendid or gloomy, jocund or unpleas-
> ant. For the passionate are naturally inclined to amplifica-
> tions; they wonderfully magnify and exaggerate whatever

dwells upon the mind. (quoted in *The Mirror and the Lamp*; my italics)

Abrams is quoting Bishop Lowth, one of the Longinians, to make the point: the mind referred to here is not the reader's but the poet's, and the classical virtue of "a plain and exact description" yields to passion and "amplifications." Figuration in particular is produced by feeling, which modifies the objects within the gaze, and Fitzgerald's extended imagery can be seen likewise to "wonderfully magnify and exaggerate":

> This is a valley of ashes—a fantastic farm where ashes
> grow like wheat into ridges and hills and grotesque gardens:
> where ashes take the forms of houses and chimneys and
> rising smoke and, finally, with a transcendent effort, of ash-
> gray men who move dimly and already crumbling through
> the powdery air.

The importance of image, from this vantage, derives less from what is seen through the lens and more from the smudges left on it—in Fitzgerald's case, an aesthetic judgment that implies a moral one. The passage washes over us like music. Or like poetry, one might say, since

> [i]n so far as a literary product simply imitates objects, it is
> not poetry at all. As a result, reference of poetry to the exter-
> nal universe disappears . . . except to the extent that sensible
> objects may serve as a stimulus or occasion for . . . poetry.
> "The poetry is not in the object itself," but "in the state of
> mind" in which it is contemplated. When a poet describes a
> lion he "is describing the lion professedly, but the statement
> of excitement of the spectator really," and the poetry must be
> true not to the object but to "the human emotion." (Abrams,
> quoting John Stuart Mill)

Lyric poetry, certainly, already so closely allied with feeling, would be less than ever obliged to the plausible, the ordinary.

Consider, for instance, this "expressive" statement:

Poppies

Little poppies,
Do you do no harm?

I cannot touch you.
And it exhausts me to watch you . . .

There are fumes that I cannot touch.
Where are your opiates, your capsules?

If your liquors could seep to me, in this glass capsule,
Dulling and stilling.

The tone is clear enough—erotic, tender, a bit impatient. What is missing is motivation: we don't know why the speaker is seduced by, or seducing, the flowers, and our participation is foreclosed. This will not be helped much by restoring the purely descriptive or representational figures, those images that provide a "reproduction in the mind of a sensation produced by a physical perception":

Poppies in July

Little poppies, little flames,
Do you do no harm?

You flicker. I cannot touch you.
I put my hands among the flames. Nothing burns.

And it exhausts me to watch you
Flickering like that, wrinkly and clear red.

There are fumes that I cannot touch.
Where are your opiates, your capsules?

If your liquors could seep to me, in this glass capsule,
Dulling and stilling.

Poppies are now *flames, flickering,* . . . *wrinkly and clear red*, but to what extent is this an "ostensible copy or replica"? Even the imagery seems "earnest to display" not some recognizable blossoms from the external universe but a mind agitated and obsessed. Here is Sylvia Plath's actual poem, from *Ariel*, with all its imagery and figuration restored:

Poppies in July

Little poppies, little hell flames,
Do you do no harm?

You flicker. I cannot touch you.
I put my hands among the flames. Nothing burns.

And it exhausts me to watch you
Flickering like that, wrinkly and clear red, like the skin of a
    mouth.

A mouth just bloodied.
Little bloody skirts!

There are fumes that I cannot touch.
Where are your opiates, your nauseous capsules?

If I could bleed, or sleep!—
If my mouth could marry a hurt like that!

Or your liquors seep to me, in this glass capsule,
Dulling and stilling.

But colourless. Colourless.

It is not very far from the Romantics' view that "the objects signified by a poem . . . were no more than a projected equivalent . . . for the poet's inner state of mind," to the practice of symbolists "from Baudelaire through T. S. Eliot" (Abrams). Eliot, however, retreated an important distance from "amplifications" that "wonderfully magnify and exaggerate," endorsing instead a set of objects, a situation, a chain of events which shall be the formula of that *particular* emotion; such that when the external facts, which must terminate in sensory experience, are given, the emotion is immediately evoked. If you examine any of Shakespeare's most successful tragedies, you will find this exact equivalence[;] . . . the state of mind of Lady Mac-Beth has been communicated to you by a skillful accumulation of imagined sensory impressions. ("Hamlet and His Problems," in *The Sacred Wood*)

With the "objective correlative," Bishop Lowth's "sensations" are made "sensory," his "turbid stream" constrained by a "skillful accumulation," the expressive impulse embodied in "external facts." And the new formula held with impressive longevity.

Plath no doubt read Eliot's essays, and perhaps read them again or recalled them the last year of her life when she wrote home jubilantly that she'd found a way to do it—to write poems directly from her own exhilarated, defeated, swirling emotional state. In poem after poem it is the image that tries to mediate between poet and page, between page and reader, to articulate the interior landscape and weather which are her subject. That penultimate and figurative verb, for instance, *marry*, doesn't enter "Poppies in July" by accident. In July she was burning Ted Hughes's letters and papers while he was in London, probably for a tryst. In September, as the death poems began to take shape at an astonishing rate, she had, she told friends, "thrown Ted out." The autobiographical circumstance infuses everything, muddying the lens—*hell flames? the skin of a mouth? a mouth just bloodied? bloody skirts?* The size, color, and texture of the poppies shift, veer, as in nightmare, and the very discrepancy between these poppies and "real" or familiar poppies makes the imagery an efficient means to dramatize the speaker in distress, much as Lady MacBeth's incessant handwashing does. Nor does the idiosyncrasy of her figures necessarily make them decorative or indulgent; they are the weight-bearing walls of the lyric structure.

If the poem succeeds, this is because what might otherwise be abstract or private or alien—the speaker's desperation—floating between us and the impress in our minds of actual poppies like a cluster of eye-motes, establishes the persona: that is, it works dramatically, as Frost defined the term—"easily heard as sung or spoken by a person in a scene." And if it fails, it fails dramatically: the persona remains too idiosyncratic or inarticulate.

Not all of us, of course, are as intent as the confessional poets on "describing the lion professedly, but the state of excitement of the spectator really"; nor, however, can we still naively divide mind (abstraction, idea, concept) from body or, post-Heisenberg, the object seen from the observer seeing it. Even in the "sort of poetry where painting or sculpture seems as if it were 'just coming over into speech,'" the image, for Pound, was both firmly allied with "examination of truth" and defined as an "intellectual and emotional complex in an instant of time." More recently, Thom Gunn praised Christopher Isherwood's "power of objective perception" this way:

> Too much has been made of his phrase "I am a camera," as
> Isherwood himself knew, but nevertheless—given the fact
> that humans are creatures of almost uncontrollable bias—
> a camera is not a bad thing to emulate. Even the practice
> of analogy is not completely un-camera-like: cameras often
> record that one thing resembles another, a church is like
> a knife, for instance, or foam on a brown stream like stout.
> The attempt to represent with clarity is always worth making,
> however impossible it is to achieve in absolute terms. (We
> may call the attempt "fairness.") There is no danger of the
> writer's ever turning into a real camera, but the imitation of
> the camera may be good training. And its faithfulness of attention to physical imagery is valuable because through it we
> may learn about the appearance of the world outside of us, or
> in other words about things we didn't know before. Doing so
> helps us to escape from the singleness of our minds, which,

if lived in exclusively, become prisons. ("Christopher Isherwood: Getting Things Right")

Exteriority is reasserted here, and precision over magnification,
but with a wistfulness: the imitative project is now a moral issue,
"the attempt to represent with clarity" recognized as "impossible . . . to achieve in absolute terms." The classical function of
the image remains—it records the dependable concrete nouns
of our common reality, uncovering the congruence among them
—but one is not surprised by the fog of the individual sensibility settling down around the lens, as in the following poem by
Theodore Roethke.

Child on Top of a Greenhouse

The wind billowing out the seat of my britches,
my feet crackling splinters of glass and dried putty,
the half-grown chrysanthemums staring up like accusers,
up through the streaked glass, flashing with sunlight,
a few white clouds all rushing eastward,
a line of elms plunging and tossing like horses,
and everyone, everyone pointing up and shouting!

There seems in the poem a genuine "attempt to represent with
clarity" (*splinters of glass and dried putty, streaked glass, flashing
with sunlight, a few white clouds*). There is a movie camera here
too, recording action in present participles that agitate the long
sentence fragment (*wind billowing out, feet crackling splinters, a
line of elms plunging and tossing, everyone pointing up and shouting*). But there's also something else: a human figure (*my britches,
my feet*), and thereby what Gunn calls, with a certain ironic pleasure, "uncontrollable bias," pulling the poem away from imitation, toward dramatization. *Half-grown chrysanthemums staring
up like accusers* is both representational, in that it seems a vivid
and precise rendering of actual flowers growing in the greenhouse, AND expressive, because a child doing something forbid-

den and risky would have seen them that way. *A line of elms plunging and tossing like horses* is a plausible "relict of a known sensation" (as I. A. Richards defines image), but it also articulates, in its rhythm and figure, the rush of exhilaration experienced by the child, the freedom from and even power over the others, whose attention he has secured while remaining firmly out of their reach.

According to Susanne Langer, in *Philosophy in a New Key*, "A subject which has emotional meaning for the artist may thereby rivet his attention and cause him to see its form with a discerning, active eye, and to keep that form present in his excited imagination until its highest reaches of significance are evident to him." This is what she calls "presentational apperception," and it at least addresses, in ways that conventional notions of the image do not, the extent to which Roethke's realistic images of the greenhouse feel totemic, like Plath's poppies or bees retrieved from the "image-cellar, dream-bank" (Seamus Heaney's terms). The contrasting similes (*like accusers, like horses*) and the crucial adjective *half-grown* seem not accidentally coincidental to both vegetation and child. They function as lyric signals in a way that parallels those moments of intensification in the syntax: *staring up like accusers,/UP through the streaked glass,* and *everyone, EVERYONE pointing up and shouting!*

For the contemporary lyric poet of classical OR Romantic affinity, then, the most useful function of the image would seem to be less imitation than dramatization. That is, image can supply not only what the writer-as-camera uncovers in the empirical world, or what the writer-as-ecstatic isolates and articulates from the whirl of the individual psyche, but the moment when both are fused in objects seen, heard, smelled, and rendered with human response still clinging to them. Langer says:

> A mind that works primarily with meanings must have organs that supply it primarily with forms. . . . [T]he world of sense is the *real world construed by the abstractions* which the sense-organs immediately furnish [my italics].

The abstractions made by the ear and the eye—the forms of direct perception— . . . are genuine symbolic materials, media of understanding, by whose office we apprehend a world of things, and of events that are the histories of things. To furnish such conceptions is their prime mission. . . .

. . . But the laws that govern visual articulation are altogether different from the laws of syntax that govern language. The most radical difference is that visual forms are not discursive. They do not present their constituents successively, but simultaneously, so the relations determining a visual structure are grasped in one act of vision.

The power of an image, in a literary work, derives largely from its own essential paradox—a "picture in words" articulates a nondiscursive apperception through the discursive systems of language—which reflects the paradox of human consciousness: the fact that mind IS body, whether sense organs or cerebrum. The most effective images, then, may be those in which the two opposing poles, the two ends of that mind/body spectrum, are collapsed in on themselves. Such images duplicate what Langer calls "presentational logic," delivering simultaneously the concrete and the abstract, the empirical and the assumed, the representational and the expressive.

We need not, in other words, be trapped in a historical dichotomy we have since outgrown, one that perhaps inhered, for notions of the image, in constrictions of the term "imitation" as customarily mistranslated from the Greek *mimesis*, which had "a different and somewhat broader range of meaning than the English word. Ultimately derived from mimos, which in the historical period denoted the 'mime' or an actor therein, mimesis seems to have meant originally the mimicking of a person or creature through dance, facial expression, and/or speech and song. But the object so 'imitated' might be a god, a mythical hero, or a fabulous creature, e.g., the Minotaur: in other words, mimesis could refer to an idea" (*Princeton Encyclopedia*). For Aristotle,

> Epic Poetry and Tragedy, Comedy also and Dithyrambic po-
> etry, and the music of the flute and of the lyre in most of
> their forms, are all in their general conception modes of
> mimesis. [Although] they differ . . . from one another in . . .
> the manner or mode of mimesis, being in each case dis-
> tinct[,] . . . the pleasure which the poet should afford is that
> which comes from pity and fear through mimesis. (*Poetics*)

This was not the "imitation" rejected by the expressivists or a "counterfeiting of sensible reality but a presentation of univer-sals"—that is, "the permanent, characteristic modes of human thought, feeling and action" (*Princeton Encyclopedia*).

Aristotle's "allied modes" having since hardened into separate genres, the first three split off from verse (with the novel as con-temporary epic), all contemporary poets may be said to be writ-ing lyric poems. Nevertheless, his classifications and his notion of shared mimetic purpose are still helpful in examining recent poems that increasingly borrow strategies from narrative, drama, and essay or discourse. What he meant by "the pleasure . . . from pity and fear" was catharsis: the audience front-row center, the characters and actions sufficiently representational to be recog-nizable and accessible, sufficiently expressive to be enlightening and moving.

My thesis here is that the image, capable simultaneously of the "representational" and the "expressive," is a chief agent for mime-sis in a poem written for the page, and equally effective no mat-ter where the poet is located on the Gunn/Eliot spectrum, no matter how much the individual lyric may yearn for its allied modes. And it would seem, too, that the yearning occurs less be-tween two points of a straight line than around the rim of a wheel—whether one writes something Eliotic, dangerously dec-adent, architecturally formal, paradox-ridden and indirect; or seeks, with Gunn, the virtues of narrative, of a self-contained world maintained by linear plot line, direct exposition, recogniz-able concrete detail, and what could pass as "objective perception." For contemporary poetry, which seems to travel at will from one genre allegiance to another, the more crucial division may lie with the vertical coordinates: the highly presentational and mimetic forms of drama on one side, and discourse on the other. After all, as Langer says, "the logical structures underlying all semantic functions . . . suggest a general principle of division. . . . [D]iscursive and presentational patterns show a formal difference." Frost's equivalent dictum, "Everything written is as good as it is dramatic," applies around the wheel, as I will try to demonstrate with two last poems.

Medusa

I had come to the house, in a cave of trees,
Facing a sheer sky.
Everything moved,—a bell hung ready to strike,
Sun and reflection wheeled by.

When the bare eyes were before me
And the hissing hair,
Held up at a window, seen through a door.
The stiff bald eyes, the serpents on the forehead
Formed in the air.

This is a dead scene forever now.
Nothing will ever stir.
The end will never brighten it more than this,
Nor the rain blur.

The water will always fall, and will not fall,
And the tipped bell make no sound.
The grass will always be growing for hay
Deep on the ground.

And I shall stand here like a shadow
Under the great balanced day,
My eyes on the yellow dust, that was lifting in the wind,
And does not drift away.

The structure of Louise Bogan's poem is a familiar one—the "when . . . then" arrangement of so many sonnets, cast here into past and future, then and forever. The poem opens with a narrative gesture, a past-perfect narrative summary and past-tense exposition:

> I had come to the house, in a cave of trees,
> Facing a sheer sky.
> Everything moved,—

The stanza concludes with what textbooks call two images and what I call one narrative detail and one figure:

> —a bell hung ready to strike,
> Sun and reflection wheeled by.

And the meter and rhyme are—not accidentally, I gather—those of the traditional ballad. The next stanza prepares us syntactically, and with somewhat strained description, for some event or action:

> When the bare eyes were before me
> And the hissing hair,
> Held up at a window, seen through a door.

But any unfolding narrative movement is stopped by that period, which converts the three lines to sentence fragment, just short of a real predicate and short of the satisfying completion of the alternating rhyme scheme.

Mid-stanza the little story seems to start again, with a further look at those earlier concrete nouns, eyes and hair:

> The stiff bald eyes, the serpents on the forehead
> Formed in the air.

At last the rhyme scheme has been completed (*hair/air*) and the stuttered sentence is completed—or is it? Is *formed* in fact only a past participle? If so, the entire stanza lacks an actual predicate, lacks the verb essential to story, since story is so thoroughly caught in time; if not, what a curiously inactive and abstract predicate it is. The narrative is left hanging, made subordinate by the syntax, and the literal, physical detail suddenly seems, well, figurative—eyes aren't usually *bald*, and hair doesn't hiss. As it happens, the image formed here is entirely referential—"conceptions burst[ing] out"—to the Medusa head of myth: to idea.

As it happens, that's all we get for "then"; the climactic event is curiously blacked out. We open the third stanza with what our encyclopedia calls abstraction, in three declarative independent clauses. The first, with its passive construction, provides the only present moment in the poem, as a pivot: *This is a dead scene forever now*. The next two follow *forever* into the future tense, which will dominate the poem's last half:

> Nothing will ever stir.
> The end will never brighten it more than this.

At exactly the place where a good narrative would deliver its complicating action, where the cameras should roll, where literal, concrete, sensuous, representational images seem most appropriate and necessary, Bogan eschews them. But somewhere in our recessed reptilian brains we've registered that the meter of the lines duplicates the opening stanza: initial irregular tetrameter, followed by a fully end-stopped trimeter, then a third line of rough iambic pentameter, and finally a shorter end-stopped line that delivers the rhyme (*Nor the rain blur*). It is as if she were starting over—and in a way she is, going back as she does to the dramatic setting. But what we get next is not story, not a sequence of events or actions, but two stanzas of imagery. First, a return to the same scene in the continuous future, with successive declarative sentences and the most active predicates thus far:

> The water will always fall, and will not fall,
> And the tipped bell make no sound.
> The grass will always be growing for hay
> Deep on the ground.

And then the focus turns back to the speaker, the "I" who opened the poem, Medusa's victim, in one sensuous sentence:

> And I shall stand here like a shadow
> Under the great balanced day,
> My eyes on the yellow dust, that was lifting in the wind,
> And does not drift away.

If the poem starts with Gunn's restrained camera, it moves subsequently into Eliot's objective correlative, and the bell's recurrence marks it for us. A *bell hung ready to strike* is a "relict of a known sensation," a familiar bell, an empirical bell; a *tipped bell* that makes no sound is not—it does not exist in the physical world. Concrete, sensual, and specific, the water, bell, grass, shadow, and yellow dust can also be called "idea-bearing," dependent as they are on the Medusa myth even to make sense; suggestive as they are of other sorts of paralysis of the will, a recurrent subject of Bogan's; congenial as they are to the general dilemma of the lyric poet. Though taxonomy may be of limited use, I think of them as dramatic images, distinguishable from the detail (house, cave of trees), description (*a bell hung ready to strike*), and figure (*sun and reflection wheeled by, hissing hair*) of the first two stanzas. By dramatic, I mean not dramatic structure—the organization of the poem seems, rather, committed to the lyric's fixed or frozen moment—but that such images contain a presentational effectiveness.

One might counter that this effectiveness derives in the Bogan poem from an expressive impulse given over to what is, after all, a mask or assumed persona (Medusa's victim), a "represented" voice or sensibility, an actor who "mimes" or "mimics" the experience in order to produce "catharsis" in the reader/audience. A more persuasive case for dramatic imagery may come from a poem less firmly lodged in the lyric hemisphere of that circle of "allied modes," one that lacks a first-person pronoun and shares with much contemporary American verse an interest in the discursive and an essentially narrative structure. My example is from Philip Larkin, whose prose remarks about poetry would appear to place him in the Gunn/Isherwood realistic camp of "objective perception."

The Explosion

On the day of the explosion
Shadows pointed towards the pithead:
In the sun the slagheap slept.

Down the lane came men in pitboots
Coughing oath-edged talk and pipe-smoke,
Shouldering off the freshened silence.

One chased after rabbits; lost them;
Came back with a nest of lark's eggs;
Showed them; lodged them in the grasses.

So they passed in beards and moleskins,
Fathers, brothers, nicknames, laughter,
Through the tall gates standing open.

At noon, there came a tremor; cows
Stopped chewing for a second; sun,
Scarfed as in a heat-haze, dimmed.

The dead go on before us, they
Are sitting in God's house in comfort,
We shall see them face to face—

Plain as lettering in the chapels
It was said, and for a second
Wives saw men of the explosion

Larger than in life they managed—
Gold as on a coin, or walking
Somehow from the sun towards them,

One showing the eggs unbroken.

The poem is structured around a story. Stanza 1 sets the scene; stanza 2 introduces the main characters; stanza 3 offers particular and characterizing action; stanza 4 summarizes; stanza 5 provides the crucial event foretold by the title, a false or temporary climax; and stanza 7 gives the concluding action/event. Missing a first-person lyric speaker, the poem nevertheless skillfully establishes point of view with its diction—*pithead, pitboots, slagheap, moleskin, God's house*—and develops tone through the declarative, occasionally inverted syntax and the Anglo-Saxon music of spondees (*oath-edged, pipe-smoke, lark's eggs, nicknames, heathaze*).

What I want to stress is what happens in the second half—gratuitous to the narrative, essential to the poem—and how Larkin prepares us for it. The initial formal arrangement is syntactically congruent: each of the first five stanzas is end-stopped with a period, each forms a complete, rhythmically and grammatically independent sentence, each line of the tercet is at least end-paused, given syntactical integrity. But stanzas 3 and 5 differ from the others in both the sheer number of active predicates and the disjunction between line length and phrase length. Stanza 3 is the most active moment:

> One chased after rabbits; lost them;
> Came back with a nest of lark's eggs;
> Showed them; lodged them in the grasses.

Here, the poem employs its first caesuras, and the variation from established formal pattern gives the throwaway narrative moment structural importance in the poem, even as its verbs are made yet more distinct with rhythmic pattern, alliteration, and lexical repetition—*lost them . . . lark's eggs . . . showed them . . . lodged them.* Other sorts of disjunction between syntax and line occur in stanza 5, with its three predicates, where the central narrative event is triple-stitched, rendered first discursively (*At noon, there came a tremor*); then, severely enjambed, with synechdochical narrative detail (*cows / Stopped chewing for a second*); and finally, in awkward, interrupted, nonidiomatic syntax, with a descriptive or representational figure (*sun, / Scarfed as in a heat-haze, dimmed*). Three lines, three last-position caesuras, three final isolated stresses.

The triadic syntax continues into the next stanza, with the same variant (hard enjambment at the first line-end) maintaining a formal continuity that keeps the poem steady while the voice changes radically: it is the voice from the pulpit, its three clauses as openly declarative as the previous lines were formally and then syntactically strained, and the figure so far from fresh or colorful as to read as cliché:

> *The dead go on before us, they*
> *Are sitting in God's house in comfort,*
> *We shall see them face to face—*

This feels like an aside, lengthening as it does the natural pause of the held moment of the explosion and contributing nothing at all to the narrative momentum, the "story." But despite the shift in tone and verb tenses, it will prove not an interruption but an announcement of what is to follow, as if the narrator of *Our Town* had come to the edge of the stage and told us what to watch for.

What does follow is pure exposition, once again past tense:

> Plain as lettering in the chapels
> It was said, and for a second
> Wives saw men of the explosion
>
> Larger than in life they managed—

followed by the same triple-stitching used for the trauma itself—first, figure (*Gold as on a coin*); then narrative detail (*walking / Somehow from the sun towards them*); and finally dramatic image (*One showing the eggs unbroken*). Exposition amplified by detail and image: it is the strategy used in stanza 5 and gives the last three lines of the poem equal weight to the three that contain catastrophe, which is partly why they are so convincing. In addition, as with Bogan's bell we greet those eggs with a shock of recognition; they appeared early, in the most caesura-ridden stanza of the poem, the most active, the most "narrative":

> One chased after rabbits; lost them;
> Came back with a nest of lark's eggs;
> Showed them; lodged them in the grasses.

Appeared, that is, as a passing detail. And now reappear, in the last line, with the same generalizable singular pronoun (*one*), with the same uncomplicated gesture (*showed / showing* the lark's eggs), in the same matter-of-fact, understated tone, its tenderness this time extended as detail is converted into figure (*showing the eggs*—and, implicitly, the men—*unbroken*). This image provides the poem's only attempt to validate the idea at its center—that the men in fact may be in heaven, *sitting in God's house in comfort.* The poem's strategy is to let us see what the wives saw, or thought they saw. The descriptive figure (*Gold as on a coin*), by comparing the vision to something already known, already familiar, makes it vivid and clear, which is to say, makes it accessible. The descriptive detail (*walking / Somehow from the sun towards them*) yields empirical evidence, which is to say, makes it plausible. But it is with the last line that we experience pity and terror, Aristotle's catharsis; it is there that we feel what the wives felt, the grief that fuels belief and mends the exploded bodies:

> *We shall see them face to face . . .*

> One showing the eggs unbroken.

And we feel it not through exposition, or description, or narration but through the mimetic power of the final dramatic image.

On Tone

I had intended, for months, to write about clarity—as a first principle, as a life's goal. I had even set aside a clutch of my favorite poems as illustration and working text, poems that were resonant, complex, and yet clear. Then the mail brought in a bulletin, a newsletter, some of whose news was a symposium on Emily Dickinson, one of the poets in my clarity file. With more than a mild interest I turned to the appropriate pages and fixed especially on the responses to "My Life had stood—a Loaded Gun."

My Life had stood—a Loaded Gun
In Corners—till a Day
The Owner passed—identified—
And carried me away—

And now We roam in Sovereign Woods—
And now We hunt the Doe—
And every time I speak for Him—
The mountains straight reply—

And do I smile, such cordial light
Upon the Valley glow—
It is as a Vesuvian face
Had let its pleasure through—

And when at Night—Our good Day done—
I guard My Master's Head—
'Tis better than the Eider-Duck's
Deep Pillow—to have shared—

To foe of his—I'm deadly foe—
None stir the second time—
On whom I lay a Yellow Eye—
Or an emphatic Thumb—

Though I than He—may longer live
He longer must—than I
For I have but the power to kill,
Without—the power to die—

Despite the hitch in the syntax in the last stanza (it takes a while to understand the panicked insistence of *must*), this had always seemed so available to me, its dominant and recessive traits managed perfectly through six stanzas and gradually shifting in weight. The dependent speaker's almost ecstatic gratitude for rescue, for usefulness, is increasingly undermined (*speak for Him, Vesuvian face*) as she puts on knowledge with power—first seen as His, then recognized as her own, but no sooner claimed (she lays the *emphatic thumb* on the enemy in the penultimate stanza 5) than recognized as a powerlessness worse than before. And the terms of both the power and the dependency of the weapon, the tool, the partner, become more and more precise, more and more clear, until the reader recognizes that the speaker has inched so far out onto the ledge, nose to the ground, that there is no more solid ground beneath her, and we plummet, as we so often do in Dickinson, to a reversal.

But the symposium commentators pointed out the many—and complicating—subtexts. Wasn't *loaded gun* a reference to the Civil War, evidence of a socially conscious Dickinson? Or, since what's hunted is a female animal and the speaker wishes to share the pillow, aren't there gender politics at work? And how about *Sovereign* woods, the reverence for the *Master*—another of her religious poems? Perhaps it wouldn't do simply to note that each of these readings is itself a specific metaphor for the dynamic of dependency and devotion I had outlined, similar to the various stagings a director might bring to a play. Clearly, "clarity" needed some clarification. And so I passed on to my second example in the file:

Dreamsong # 29   John Berryman

There sat down, once, a thing on Henry's heart
so heavy, if he had a hundred years
& more, & weeping, sleepless, in all them time
Henry could not make good.
Starts again always in Henry's ears
the little cough somewhere, an odour, a chime.

And there is another thing he has in mind
like a grave Sienese face a thousand years
would fail to blur the still profiled reproach of. Ghastly,
with open eyes, he attends, blind.
All the bells say: too late. This is not for tears;
thinking.

But never did Henry, as he thought he did,
end anyone and hacks her body up
and hide the pieces, where they may be found.
He knows: he went over everyone, & nobody's missing.
Often he reckons, in the dawn, them up.
Nobody is ever missing.

What would a symposium think of this one? The surface of the poem lacks even the textural cleanness of the Dickinson; the syntax is anything but straightforward, is in fact deliberately contorted, delayed, elided, inverted, reeling from grammatical violation to sophisticated median appositives, as the diction likewise reels from burlesque blackface to sonorous allusion. And the plot!—can there be a narrative when nothing happens?

But despite the absence of landmarks, there is, for me, something immediate—a path, a lantern—that either passes for clarity or else gives me the patience or the willingness to make my way through the underbrush. Essentially, that "something" in John Berryman's Dreamsong #29 is a structure that inverts the Dickinson. In her poem the initial concept is developed logically, relentlessly, example after example; it is the tone, which is to say the implications suggested by the examples, that shifts. In the Berryman our initial assumption of Henry's guilt, the probable cause of something heavy on Henry's heart, is increasingly undercut, reversed, more and more frantically, down through the poem: why, he's never murdered anyone. Meanwhile, the tone, beneath the manic energy of the surface, is unwavering, the self-recrimination increasing even as convincing hard evidence for it dissipates. Whatever Henry has done to, or felt about, women, he might as well have hacked one up and hid the pieces. Such is the nature of self-loathing.

In other words, what I had meant by "clarity" had to do with "tone," with a clarity of purpose and inference more than with the discursive prose elements of a poem.

But what exactly is tone? Although crucial to the making of and reading of poems, it seems nearly impossible to define. Thrall, Hibbard, and Holman's *Handbook to Literature*, drawing directly on I. A. Richards, calls it "a term designating the attitudes toward the subject and toward the audience implied in a literary work." But this seems helpful in understanding neither the Dickinson nor the Berryman poem. *The Princeton Encyclopedia of Poetry and Poetics*, which has its own problems with tone, gives a full entry:

> Traditionally, tone has denoted an intangible quality, frequently an affective one, which is metaphorically predicated of a literary work or of some part of it such as its style. It is said to pervade and "color" the whole, like a mood in a human being, and in various ways to contribute to the aesthetic excellence of the work. . . . In *Practical Criticism*,

I. A. Richards compared tone to social manners and defined it as the reflection in a discourse of the author's attitude towards his audience.

This is not promising. Yet most of us can identify tone in *life*—and some have depended on it for survival. Tone is what we hear behind the closed door: "[t]he brute tones of our human throat," Frost said, "that may once have been all our meaning." From the volume, pitch, relative stress, pacing, and rhythmic pattern of the speech—even if the actual words are indistinct—we reconstruct the emotional content. It's what the dog registers when you talk to him sternly or playfully: the form of the emotion behind/ within the words. It's also what can allow an obscenity to pass for an endearment, or a term of affection to become suddenly an insult.

In life, what we depend on is inflection—exactly what is missing when the robot speaks. Consider this little dialogue:

—Where did you get those pants?
— On sale at Sims.
—I should have known.
—They're very comfortable.
—I'm sure they are.

On the page this exchange is what we'd call "flat"—mostly monosyllabic words, of seemingly equal importance, and foreshortened syntax that deprives us of both the relativity of subordination and the arc, or rhythmic shape, of the sentence. It may help if I provide a context, some discursive information that will encourage a reader to infer inflection (a technique used by fiction writers, particularly those writers of the "minimalist" school, who rely on flatness to suggest anomie). In this case, let's say that the pants in question are suggestive of someone's pajamas, a bright plaid in loose folds, and that the first voice is my older sister, a plausible substitute for my mother. That at least poses several options for tone, supplied by rhetorical stress. One might be solicitude alternating with resentment:

—(*inquiringly*) Where did you get THOSE pants?
—(*brusquely*) On sale at Sims.
—(*ruefully*) I should have known.
—(*aggressively*) They're VERY comfortable.
—(*agreeably*) Oh, I'm sure they are.

Another is disapproval and meek acknowledgment:

—WHERE did you GET THOSE PANTS?
—On sale, at Sims.
—I SHOULD HAVE KNOWN.
—They're very comfortable (?)
—OH   I'm SURE   they ARE.

Which is how I remember it.

The point is that the exchange, the actual language, needs a context in order for its "meaning" to be clear. A dramatic or narrative (that is, discursive) context may allow us to infer tone, but inflection—a context of sound—is more dependable. So it is, I will try to argue, with poetry as well: no matter how many discursive meanings a poem may partake of, its central meaning, or purpose, or identity, derives from its tone. As a primary text I want to use a poem by Stanley Kunitz that is more immediately accessible than either the Dickinson or the Berryman piece.

My Sisters

Who whispered, souls have shapes?
So has the wind, I say.
But I don't know,
I only feel things blow.

I had two sisters once
with long black hair
who walked apart from me
and wrote the history of tears.
Their story's faded with their names,
but the candlelight they carried,

like dancers in a dream,
still flickers on their gowns
as they bend over me
to comfort my night-fears.

Let nothing grieve you,
Sarah and Sophia.
Shush, shush, my dears,
now and forever.

Admittedly, the immediate discursive context for the poem is
a little shaky. In that opening italicized stanza we don't know
who is speaking; there seems to be no dramatic location, no event
to fasten on. And yet the poem draws us in; the tentativeness
inherent in all nonrhetorical interrogatives lets us recognize an
internalized argument with the self. Somebody—the speaker
won't or can't say who—believes in ghosts. First he dismisses the
notion (could be the wind); then he disavows a position one way
or the other (*But I don't know*) while immediately splicing into
the sentence with a comma its continued possibility (*feel things
blow*). Meanwhile, this ambivalence sets us on edge, alerts us; we
know how to feel: not terrified but uneasy.

As the poem proceeds to the next stanza, we're on firmer
ground. There is a self-proclaimed speaker, an I. The syntax is
straightforward, full declarative sentences with obvious subjects
and verbs, modifying phrases used sparingly and more or less predictably. The diction, too, poses no threat of difficulty; the words
are idiomatic, familiar. The structure is not conventional but
still seems accessible. The initial voice-from-the-ditch was italicized and thus set aside as prologue, having raised the essential
premise of the poem: do ghosts exist or not? Next we are given
the barest residue of a narrative. The speaker tells us that he had
two sisters, that they were unhappy, that they are dead, that their
spirits come to comfort him. The third stanza shifts again—this
time to direct address, the speaker now comforting the dead
sisters.

None of this "information," however, addresses the power or the effectiveness of the poem, because none of it conveys the emotional content. What does is tone, which I would argue is the source of the poem's great clarity. Even in the opening question there is more challenge than request (*who whispered*, who claimed such a thing?), and that is followed by a noticeable and almost cavalier defensiveness (*So has the wind, I say*), concomitant with both lines' disturbing, almost violent sibilance. Nine of the first eleven words share initial consonantal sounds that are full of air—*wh, w, sah, sh,* and *hah*—underscored by the medial and final *S* sounds in *whispered, souls, shapes,* and *has.* These extending consonants are then contained, as it were, by the open long *A* placed in matching stressed syllables (*shapes/say*) at the ends of the end-stopped trimeter lines. There is also a breathiness, and a serious, halting pace, introduced into the regularized meter: Kunitz puts an immediate caesura after the first foot of the poem, which reinforces the hovering possibility of an initial stress (*Who whispered*—compare that with "who whispered to me"). This potential initial stress is made authoritative in the next line (*so has the WIND*), but there the caesura is delayed; thus the rhythm of our metered three-foot couplet is varied (1 — 2, 3; 1, 2 — 3):

Who whispered, souls have shapes?
So has the wind, I say.

When the speaker then retreats a bit from his initial dismissal, the sounds likewise retreat with the shortened flat line *But I don't know*—. This line is held in tonal abeyance as the expectation of another three-beat line is thwarted, delayed just for a moment, until the next line restores trimeter in liquid *L*s (*only, feel, blow*) as the rhymes and stresses shift us down into the closed long *O*: *I only feel things blow.*

Such a weak part of speech, that adverb, *only*, so undeserving of metrical stress, but here so sly, working in the sentence as a musical transition between the *O* of *know*, the *E* of *feel*—and a slightly smug, slightly stubborn "I know what I know" creeps into the tone to complicate, if not contradict, the statement.

The edgy ambivalence of the opening stanza is relieved somewhat in stanza 2 as the voice takes up its brief weary narrative. Gone are the trimeter couplets (gone too the caesuras). But music doesn't require meter and rhyme. The *S* in *souls* in the first line carries forward to the now limited category of souls, *sisters once*, and the *L* that closed stanza 1 recurs in their *long black hair* as, in lines of increasing length, the specific dead are identified. The suggestion of rhyme scheme—an overt pattern of sound— remains in *tears/fears*, words that end and end-stop the two complete sentences of the stanza, and in the carefully placed *me/ dream/me*—as though the earlier closed couplets had been stretched open, just as the sentences and lines lengthen and relax, bulge the stanza out at its center, then return more or less to the trimeter.

Certainly, nothing in the narrative information of the second stanza (the speaker's own approaching death is the gradually emerging conflict here), nothing in the discursive context, anticipates the final shift, the role reversal in the final stanza. When the speaker turns to comfort the ghosts (who, after all, may or may not exist), the direct address, imperative syntax, and more formal diction signal the extent to which the initial doubt has been overwhelmed by tenderness: *Let nothing grieve you*. Whether or not the reader's analytical brain recognizes it, some primitive reptilian brain does: this is dimeter, the two-beat unit that surprised us earlier (*But I don't know*) and recurred in stanza 2 (*with long black hair*). Here, the duple unit uses the same iambic opening but is softened by an extra unstressed syllable, a feminine ending. With this subtle repetition and a variation even more subtle, the earlier coy disavowal is displaced, first with formal address, then immediately with the more intimate *Sarah and Sophia*. Meanwhile, the poem prepares us for closure with a four-line stanza again, to balance and resolve the initial four halting lines. This final quatrain neatly divides into syntac-

tical, if not rhymed, couplets that return us to the initial sibilance, but this time with all threat gone: *Sarah and Sophia. /
Shush, shush, my dears.* The passage is maternal, compassionate,
the speaker's own pain or fear eclipsed, turned outward.

It is tone that marks the striking difference between the last
four lines of the poem and the first four. At the onset we had
a stanza of a folk song: its set pattern of three beats, its single
duple variant, its rising rhythm, and its masculine rhyme. For
closure we have four end-stopped lines in which the earlier variation, two beats, has become the pattern, *But I don't know* res-
onating in rhythm no longer ironic, self-protective, but as dilemma: I don't know whether you're even there or not, but I bless
you anyway. Whereas the opening lines considered initial stress
and then gave way to regular iambs with masculine line endings,
this stanza pulls us back from that movement with three feminine endings (*grieve you, Sophia, forever*) and three strong initial
stresses (*Sarah, shush, now*). Because of the repeated stanzaic arrangement, we are able to detect the changes in the small strokes
(an extra syllable, a change in diction, a move from interrogative
to imperative) and thereby register the change in tone. The
stanza's falling rhythm not only departs from the dominant rising
inflection of the poem but in the last line recalls a sound pattern
from outside the poem by duplicating, after dimeter prolonged by
spondee and caesuras (*Shush, shush, my dears*), the cadence and
language of prayer:

Now and forever
[World without end].

The last word of the poem—*forever*, which is after all death's very
threat—here is converted, by the context of the sound, to a
source of promise.

It is this "plot line"—attention focused by structure and formal
arrangement on the complex and evolving emotional field—that
is the poem. It is immediately accessible; we can follow it, are engaged in it, because we hear it in the music. Even before we have

any notion of the submerged narrative, which serves as discursive context here, we register the tonality—provided by the sounds in the diction, syntax, formal manipulation of rhythm, arrangement of vowels and consonants—simultaneously with the denotative verbal information and the visual cues.

Simultaneous with—which is to say: any single element contributory to tone does not contain it. In the exchange about the pants, it would help to see the pants. When one talks to the dog, the dog also registers the familiar or unfamiliar face, smell, voice timbre, and body language. Likewise, when we hear, through the wall, voices in the next apartment, we surmise a context: whether it's a man or a woman, a child in danger, the bitchy landlord, or someone drunk; whether we should call the cops or go on to sleep. What's important is the combination of elements. This is a well-known aspect of "tonality" in music. A single note cannot truly be said to have any emotional suggestiveness at all. Even two notes in conjunction barely suggest a mode—a major third, for instance, A to $C^\sharp$, could be part of the tonic in A major or part of the 6th chord, an $F^\sharp$ minor. It's only when the third tone is added, E or $F^\sharp$, that a key or tonality is established and with it some specific color or character that makes a song different in different keys.

So any analysis of tone must include elements in conjunction with one another and, crucially, the simultaneity of those elements—voice, face, smell, body language. This is the primary distinction that Susanne Langer makes, in *Philosophy in a New Key*, between "discursive" and "presentational" modes of logic or apprehension. Discursive logic is always linear. And this is true of language itself. "Man bites dog" as a unit of syntax gives us three ideas or propositions or symbols in succession. Language can only be linear; therefore, it makes itself available to rules (syntax), to a lexicon (dictionaries supply fixed denotation—meaning that does not change in context), and to translation. Here's Langer's phrasing: "Language in the strict sense is essentially discursive; it has permanent units of meaning which are combinable into larger units; it has fixed equivalences that make definition and translation possible; its connotations are general, so that it requires nonverbal acts, like pointing, looking, or emphatic voice-inflections."

Much of what we apprehend in the world, however, does not seem linear, one item at a time, but simultaneous, what Langer calls presentational. The senses function that way. When we witness a painting, or a man biting a dog, the elements of the visual image impress themselves simultaneously; it is only the need to verbalize them that makes them linear. A nondiscursive symbol

> is composed of elements that represent various respective constituents in the object; but these elements are not units with independent meanings. The areas of light and shade that constitute a portrait have no significance by themselves. In isolation we would consider them simply blotches. Yet they are faithful representatives of visual elements composing the visual object. . . . We may well pick out some line, say a certain curve, in a picture, which serves to represent one nameable item; but in another place the same curve would have an entirely different meaning. It has no fixed meaning apart from its context. (Langer)

Surely we're not interested in poems that content themselves with only discursive experience for the reader. To a large extent, even though as language objects poems must release themselves discursively, and even though some of them undertake the discursive tasks of narrative or argument, history or philosophy, the best poems of any mode become nondiscursive symbols. That is, syntax and diction work not only to convey discursive information, not only as "rules" and denotative items from the lexicon, but also to duplicate, with their sounds, something of the inflection we respond to, in life, non-discursively. Isn't this what we're after? "[V]erbal symbolism . . . has primarily a general reference. . . . In the non-discursive mode that speaks directly to sense, however, there is no intrinsic generality. It is first and foremost a direct presentation of an individual object" (Langer). If the "object" is experience rendered by the poem, then all the sounds of the poem—and in particular patterns of sound, since these impress themselves more indelibly on the ear—work as a unified or common context (totality) AGAINST the necessarily linear movement of word after word after word.

> The meanings given through language are successively understood, and gathered into a whole by the process called discourse; the meanings of all other symbolic elements that compose a larger articulate symbol are understood only through the meaning of the whole, through their relations within the total structure. Their very functioning . . . depends on the fact that they are involved in a simultaneous, integral presentation. (Langer)

For a poem to become that "larger articulate symbol," context is crucial. There is no fixed emotional equivalent for any particular vowel sound, no matter its high or low "frequency" (*pace* J. F. Nims), nor any given metrical pattern (*pace* Alexander Pope), nor any particular syntactical arrangement (compare Plath's assaultive questions to Hopkins's plaintive ones). A fast song is not necessarily happier than a slow one. If anapests seem to murmur, it's because the statement as well as the sound of the statement suggests the murmuring. And when we hear tenderness in Kunitz's address, it comes from the sound as applied to the information already released: our knowledge that Sarah and Sophia are the speaker's sisters, and long dead. At the same time, it does seem true that context in a poem is built less often from narrative or expository elements, which are required by the nature of language to be linear or discursive, and more often, more easily, more effectively from elements that appeal most directly to the senses, those instruments for gathering presentational information. Poetry derives, that is, from music and from imagery.

In much of her discussion Langer relies on painting, on the visual and nonverbal, to develop her distinction between discursive and presentational apprehension, and one thinks as well of the sensory power of images in a poem. Certainly, Kunitz's visual cues do establish context and reinforce the tone: the long black hair, the flickering candlelight, the bending figures are of a piece with the suggestion of something extraordinary lodged in the heightened folk music of the opening, the initial question and consequent evocation of the elements, the broad strokes of the narrative, even the abstract end-stopped phrase *history of tears*. But I wonder if they are sufficient, without the supporting score, to establish tone—if, in fact, they aren't rather predictable ghost-story trappings which, when isolated, might evoke either a sentimental or a cynical response.

There may be other poems that depend more heavily on imagery to establish and convey tone; one thinks in particular of poetry in translation—the French poet Jean Follain, for example—where the images seem to function as, say, a narrative or dramatic context might function, absorbing some of the contribution usually made by inflection. But the case of Sylvia Plath and her indelible imagery seems to suggest otherwise. Diary entries recording the death and funeral of a neighbor in June 1962 rely on observed visual details that turn up again in subsequent poems—but with markedly different tonal implications. Even the difference between the diary entry below and its appropriation five days later into "Berck-Plage" is instructive: that is, although the imagery recurs, there is a tonal difference between the prose excerpt with its discursive context and clear if reductive exposition (it made me sick, it was a horror) and the poem with its musical context and tonal complexity, its sense of exhilarating release and fascination.

> Percy lay back on a heap of white pillows in his striped pajamas, his face already passed from humanity, the nose a spiraling, fleshless beak in thin air, the chin fallen in a point from it, like an opposite pole, and the mouth like an inverted black heart stamped into the yellow flesh between, a great raucous breath coming and going there with great effort like

an awful bird. . . . His eyes showed through partly open lids like dissolved soaps or a clotted pus. I was very sick at this and had a bad migraine over my left eye for the rest of the day. The end, even of so marginal a man, a horror. . . .

When I went down they had just brought the coffin and put him in. The living room where he had lain was in an up-heaval—bed rolled from the wall, mattresses on the lawn, sheets and pillows washed and airing. He lay in the sewing room, or parlor, in a long coffin of orangey soap-colored oak[,] . . . the lid propped against the wall at his head with a silver scroll: Percy B, Died June 25, 1962. The raw date a shock. A sheet covered the coffin. Rose lifted it. A pale white, beaked face, as of paper, rose under the veil that covered the hole cut in the glued white cloth cover. The mouth looked glued, the face powdered. (*Johnny Panic and the Bible of Dreams*)

(II)

This black boot has no mercy for anybody.
Why should it, it is the hearse of a dead foot,

The high, dead, toeless foot of this priest . . .

(IV)

A wedding-cake face in a paper frill.
How superior he is now.

. . . The bed is rolled from the wall.

This is what it is to be complete. It is horrible.
Is he wearing pajamas or an evening suit

Under the glued sheet from which his powdery beak
Rises so whitely unbuffeted? . . .

Now the washed sheets fly in the sun,
The pillow cases are sweetening.

It is a blessing, it is a blessing:
The long coffin of soap-coloured oak,

The curious bearers and the raw date
Engraving itself in silver with marvelous calm.

(VI)

The voice of the priest, in thin air,
Meets the corpse at the gate,

Addressing it, while the hills roll the notes of the dead bell;
A glitter of wheat and crude earth.

(From "Berck-Plage," June 30, 1962)

If the same image, in the same situational context, can command different emotional implications, then images are not a dependable source of tone in a poem. Perhaps this is because we receive them through the linear arrangement of language, as though given first a swatch of red, then a straight black line, which we must piece together to re-create the painting. Most probably, we are responding as much to an abstraction of or symbolic quality within the object as to some actual visualization of that object. Sound, on the other hand, provides the simultaneity Langer stresses. Alter the sounds even slightly in the Kunitz poem—make it read "Shush, my dears" or "Hush hush, my dears"—and the tone wobbles. Thus, despite the importance of each of the elements contributing to the overall "tonality" of a poem, I have come to believe that the best poems, even discursive poems of narrative or argument, build their tonal context primarily through their sounds.

Let me stop to summarize. In a poem an event or idea has been verbalized—cast into discursive logic—and we respond with a discursive linear logic to the statements made. But we are also responding to, registering, the combined and simultaneous effect of those presentational elements that produce a "tonality" or musical key. It is this simultaneity that makes it so difficult to isolate the source of tone in a poem—that, and the need to break down the presentational apprehension of it into the linear or discursive logic of language when we try to talk about it. Nonetheless, I am making a case that tone is located most often, most dependably, in sound, a nondiscursive context apart from though simultaneous with the discursive information provided. I say "apart from" because we can hear when the two are in conflict or opposition— as, for instance, in Larkin's notable poem "This Be the Verse"— and call it irony.

Thus, I might formulate the following hypothesis:

> that the best poems also function as nondiscursive symbols, in addition to their discursive purposes;
> that the nondiscursive logic operates through tone;
> that tone itself is primarily lodged in and conveyed by the sounds of the poem, both gross motor (pattern and repetition, sentence and line) and fine motor (syllable, vowel, and consonant);
> that disregard of the music of the poem, or application of only its technical apparatus (such as fixed meter and rhyme scheme), particularly in poems already heavily discursive in mode and structure, leads to a loss or disturbance of tone, and with that loss comes a loss of clarity;
> and, conversely, that if the tone is so entirely expected, or conventional, as to admit no friction between subject and the sensibility perceiving it, the poem is diminished.

"The sensibility perceiving it": are we back, then, to the old dichotomy of thought versus feeling? Not according to Langer: "A subject which has emotional meaning for the artist may thereby rivet his attention and cause him to see its form with a discerning, active eye, and to keep that form present in his excited imagination until its highest reaches of significance are evident to him; then he will have, and will paint, a deep and original conception of it."

The presentational logic of the poem, it should be stressed, is not so much self-expression of emotions felt by the artist as it is his or her grasp of the form of the emotion: "not 'self-expression'" but "exposition of feelings . . . expressing primarily the artist's knowledge of human feeling, not how or when that knowledge was acquired" (Langer). It is the form of the emotion that is embodied in the formal expression or arrangements of the text, where, as Kunitz has put it, "line-by-line progression of subtle harmonies and discords [corresponds] with variable states of feeling" (*Next-to-Last Things*).

It is my purpose here to contradict Richards's notion that tone emanates from the poet's "attitude toward the audience," a matter that seems to me an element of style more than of tone. Essentially, attitude toward audience is part of the fixed persona of the poet—fixed, that is, within an aesthetic position that may shift over time but contains or reflects overall self-presentation. In a single volume of poems we find an identifiable "style" that is applied to various subjects and thereby adheres to the poet, rather than to the material. Sufficiently consistent through a lifetime, it becomes the thumbprint of the writer. And sometimes the style is sufficiently idiosyncratic, or sufficiently concomitant with what biography confirms as inherent personality, that a characteristic tone becomes a part of that style. In Elizabeth Bishop, for instance, the caution, the decorum, betrayed by her hesitancy, exactness of detail, understatement, and parenthetical syntax within a rough trimeter call to mind "Bishop" as much as hearing her actual voice would. This last seems the set of manners toward one's audience that Richards must have had in mind.

But, I would argue, there is no necessary connection between style and tone. We can compare, for instance, several of the *Ariel* poems written in the last weeks of Plath's life, treating of the same subject: her past suicide attempt and the increasing attractiveness of death as a renewed option. The style of these poems is remarkably unified: the exaggerated comparisons, the severe enjambment of sonorous passages, the punch of declarative sentences yoked by commas or fully end-stopped as the pitch of the frenzy requires, and the dramatic description. Many of the same images recur, such as the boot, the toe, the bell, the beak, the lifted linen seen first in the diary entries and poem (quoted above) about a neighbor's death. Nevertheless, the tone is remarkably different in "Daddy" (October 12), "Lady Lazarus" (October 21), "Ariel" (October 27), "Death & Co." (November 14), and "The Edge" (February 4), moving respectively from hysterical rage to puerile revenge to ecstatic escape to cool resignation to —finally, in "The Edge"—a kind of sympathy or forgiveness toward the self, now as distanced as the unaffiliated corpse in "Berck-Plage."

The source of these differences in tone seems not the poet's "attitude toward her audience" but her apprehension of the subject. Apprehension: no neat little division between the hard empirical fact of the subject and warm runny ooze of the poet's "feelings"; rather, subject as perceived and then rendered presentationally, the form of the emotion in its own logic. And a resulting tension is provided to the poem in part by the discrepancy between unchallenged (that is, conventional) understanding of the subject and the "deep and original perception of it" that Langer cited.

I'd like, then, to offer my own rough definition, by way of Langer: *Tone in a poem expresses the form of the emotion in that poem and is lodged primarily in the poem's nondiscursive elements, especially in its music. Music is meant here to include both the broad units of repetition, sentence structure, and lineation and the small units of syllable, vowel, and consonant. As with "tonality" in a composition, tone instructs the attention of, first, the poet, then the reader, through a context of sounds working either with or against the discursive elements of the poem, and it may itself be an element of either unity or energy (plot) within the piece.*

The discursive possibilities in poetry are what currently most absorb many contemporary poets, whether writers engaged in personal or historical narrative, Neoformalists wielding the technical apparatus of traditional verse, or even "language poets" radically celebrating the sequential or linear nature of language by widening the synapses between units. With theorists busy separating reference from its tonal context, with poets' own natural aversion to the extremity of the subjective that we saw in Plath and Berryman, with the perception of a diminishing or alienated audience for poetry, with discomfort over the reductiveness of the domestic or personal I, and with the makers' wish for a greater capaciousness, poets are eager to redefine the nature of poetry—to "make it new." But a redefinition toward the linear risks the loss not only of power but of clarity. Langer is firm: "The logical structures underlying all semantic functions . . . suggest a general principle of division. . . . [D]iscursive and presentational patterns show a formal difference."

Or, as W. B. Yeats put it in 1906, in the afternoon of another discursive age: "Art bids us touch and taste and hear and see the world, and shrinks from what Blake calls mathematic form, from every abstract thing, from all that is of the brain only, from all that is not a fountain jetting from the entire hopes, memories, and sensations of the body" (*Essays and Introductions*).

Structural Subversion

Poet and novelist Stephen Dobyns has said that every lyric poem implies a narrative. What he means is a sequence of past events, left out of the poem, that brought the speaker to the present, intensified moment in the poem. Assuming the speaker is the poet, Dobyns also means autobiography—if not an actual experience, then the life story informing the utterance, bleeding through in tone or quirky detail. Implicit in his observation is a wish for more information, more context than a densely musical text can accommodate. It's a preference that speculates over dinner about the couple at the next table, inventing identity and circumstance on the spot, or later at the novel-making desk, deducing either from the limited evidence of what was witnessed or from experience. Increasingly, it would seem also to be the preference of readers in our neo-narrative age, age of biography and memoir, age of the talk show: an appetite for story.

But the lyric poet might just as easily say that every narrative poem obscures a lyric. What I mean is the stone in the stream, the single suggestive gesture or perception or response that crystallizes and embodies the subterranean life, the other world beneath the surface of this one. The man in the restaurant crushing a wineglass in his hand acts out an emotional complex not wholly explained by a hard day at the office, or being cheated in the taxi, or what his companion just said. If the narrative writer is instinctively curious about the individuating "story," is hard-wired for the distinct sequence of events preceding that table and that wineglass, the lyric poet may be as naturally drawn to the isolated human moment of frustration, distilled, indelible, the peak in the emotional chart.

I once showed Dobyns a draft of a first-person poem that opens on a couple reading in bed, a rustle in the cold woodstove. After a stanza of scene there is a descriptive stanza as a creature emerges—not the bird they had imagined but a bat; then two italicized lines, voice-from-the-ditch, introducing compressed, generalized action as they kill it and call in the cat for disposal. Dobyns's assessment: You haven't said how they killed the bat. True enough—I hadn't, and it seemed, when he pointed it out, a reparable weakness. But as Charles Wright has noted about himself, just because I was from the South didn't mean I could tell a story. Fifty drafts later I still hadn't said how they killed the bat. I tried a broom, a tennis racket, a flung pillow. None was apt; the new language had no spark; the specificity contributed nothing.

There were two problems with the proposed solution. First: I didn't CARE how they killed the bat; I was not sufficiently engaged by the permutations of character and circumstance to imagine it fully. More problematic was that how they killed it had no *consequence*: I had no "story" to tell. What interested me lay wholly in the quick reversal from mellow speculation to panic, from passive sympathy for trapped fellow creature to instinctive loathing of the alien, from the civilized (reading in bed) to the primitive (gotta get rid of that bat). In the poem, scene and characters function only to prepare the reader to feel what they felt when they saw the bat; the action was denouement, and elaborated action not only unessential but a distraction from the single juxtaposition: bat alive and swooping, then bat bashed—no discrimination among degrees of violence.

Shortly thereafter, I set myself the task of learning how to tell a story, how to watch for consequential junctures of fate and will, but I had to do it in another book, with other subjects, in which sequence was crucial—"and then," "and then," "and then," real alternatives closing out and others opening for subsequent choice or action or event. And while I was beginning that project (*The Lotus Flowers*), I was again confronted with my intentions in the bat poem. Isn't that poem, an interviewer said, quintessentially southern, given its focus on family, its presentation of a violent natural world, its biblical/religious reference, and especially its use of *narrative*?

There must be books that explain in convincing detail why the South is, as Flannery O'Connor says, "a storytelling section." Sometimes what the observer means is a society's civil comportment: grocery traffic halts at the checkout counter while the employee at the register pauses to tell the story of her aunt's surgery to the customer next in line. Sometimes what is meant is fiction's dominance over poetry in the southern canon, not only in the early and Confederate South but following the modern "Southern Renaissance." The Scott, Foresman anthology *The Literature of the South*, the text for my college class in southern literature in 1963 (as it probably had been for my professor a decade earlier at Vanderbilt) selects work from four "Poets and Critics" since 1918: John Crowe Ransom, Donald Davidson, Allen Tate, and Randall Jarrell. For "Prose Fiction" of the same period: Ellen Glasgow, Stark Young, Elizabeth Madox Roberts, Katherine Anne Porter, Caroline Gordon, Andrew Lytle, Jesse Stuart, Eudora Welty, Carson McCullers, Peter Taylor, Truman Capote, Flannery O'Connor, and Shirley Ann Grau. Richard Wright shows up in a cultural commentary section, and "Three Representative Authors" end the volume: Thomas Wolfe, William Faulkner, and Robert Penn Warren, the last represented by two stories and four poems (including the thoroughly narrative "Ballad of Billie Potts").

If there is in the region a cultural compatibility with narrative, the imbalance in its literature seems natural enough. Narrative since Homer, lacking epic subject, has increasingly found a better location in fiction, where there is room to develop and reveal character, acting and acted upon over time. Making character known also needs idiom, and prose more easily sustains the idiomatic (all those unstressed syllables in speech rhythms—by the pond, under the tree, after the dance); in poetry, whose first allegiance must be to music, nothing wears so quickly as the flat line. But southern writers have also been instrumental in the wholesale reemergence of narrative in contemporary American poetry, restoring an audience for it by the by, and any recent anthology of southern literature contains their work: James Dickey, Fred Chappell, Dave Smith, James Applewhite, David Bottoms, Henry Taylor, David Huddle, Rodney Jones, Leon Stokesbury, T. R. Hummer, Andrew Hudgins, Brooks Haxton, and others. Definition follows practice; additional application follows definition. Even this sketchy account is, of course, itself a kind of story—How Southern Poetry Got to Be So Narrative. Or: How I Wrestled Faulkner to the Ground. Poor little bat.

So what does that make Charles Wright, Donald Justice, A. R. Ammons, Eleanor Ross Taylor, and much of Betty Adcock, other than the exceptions to prove the rule? Out on a far branch of the family tree, wasn't there some subversive progenitor?

> Once upon a midnight dreary, while I pondered, weak and
>   weary,
> Over many a quaint and curious volume of forgotten lore,
> While I nodded, nearly napping, suddenly there came a
>   tapping
> As of some one gently rapping, rapping at my chamber door.
> "'Tis some visitor," I muttered, "tapping at my chamber
>   door—
> Only this and nothing more."

It's a ghost story, of course, and also a prototype for current "personal narrative" in American poetry. Poet/speaker is up late reading, or trying to read, grieving actually for "the lost Lenore," rare and radiant—and dead—maiden. Bird knocks at the window, speaker lets him in, and conversation ensues (more or less—the bird really doesn't hold up his end, although the progressive hysteria of the speaker compensates). The structure here is didactic: from the fairytale opening to the last *Nevermore*, almost every stanza carries at least one direct time reference (*midnight, bleak December, now, presently, Soon again, Then, Then, Then, Then*) and action (*I wished, I stood repeating, I opened wide the door, I whispered, I heard, I flung the shutter, Raven . . . perched* and *sat*).

But Poe has built a fort to house a butterfly: there is no "story"; nothing happens. Look at the predicates, once the bird has entered: *quoth, marveled, spoke, muttered, said, cried, quoth, said, implore, quoth, said, quoth, shrieked, quoth*. What follows the bird's appearance is the rising line of despair and its corollary, the increasingly maddening vacuity of the bird's non-response. That the Raven doesn't attack, or say anything else, or fly away is what keeps it an emblem of both the speaker's distress and the failure of the world, civilized and natural, to alleviate that distress. Meanwhile, Poe's obsessive, sound-drunk ear provides the claustrophobic emotional field, having doubled the ballad conventions: the characteristic four-beat metric and its trimeter variation are recalled by interior rhymes (*dreary/weary, napping/ tapping*); the end rhymes are kept in the traditional alternating pattern (*weary/lore/tapping/door*); and the refrain tortures us with its unvaried, unrelieved single note—*Nevermore*. Despite its rigid narrative gestures, "The Raven" is lyric in its deepest purposes, and "our cousin, Mr. Poe," as Tate called him, is the wellhead I was looking for in what I've come to think of as structural subversion.

In their introduction to *Southern Writing in the Sixties: Poetry* (1967), John William Corrington and Miller Williams refer to the slow evolution of poetry, relative to fiction, in nineteenth-century New England.

Just so in the South the field has belonged generally to the
storytellers. Until the third decade of this century, the names
of John Esten Cooke, Thomas Nelson Page, George Washington Cable, John Chandler Harris, and Ellen Glasgow, clearly
no Melvilles, had no counterparts in poetry, unless we consider Edgar Allan Poe, and perhaps Sidney Lanier. The
Southerner was getting a reputation as a good story teller,
but the poets were then in Concord or Boston or New York.

Then something happened. And what happened was John
Crowe Ransom.

We know a handful of Ransom's poems fairly well, lyrics and
narratives, particularly "Captain Carpenter," a ballad as arch as
Poe's was earnest, and "Janet Waking," where the irony falls
somewhere shy of satire under pressure of sympathy for the protagonist. Less well anthologized are his genre-straddling structural subversions, such as "Vision by Sweetwater":

Go and ask Robin to bring the girls over
To Sweetwater, said my Aunt; and that was why
It was like a dream of ladies sweeping by
The willows, clouds, deep meadowgrass, and the river.

Robin's sisters and my Aunt's lily daughter
Laughed and talked, and tinkled light as wrens
If there were a little colony all hens
To go walking by the steep turn of Sweetwater.

Let them alone, dear Aunt, just for one minute
Till I go fishing in the dark of my mind:
Where have I seen before, against the wind,
These bright virgins, robed and bare of bonnet,

Flowing with music of their strange quick tongue
And adventuring with delicate paces by the stream,—
Myself a child, old suddenly at the scream
From one of the white throats which it hid among?

The first sentence is the paradigm. The opening line hovers midway, like Anglo-Saxon accentual verse, then slides across the enjambment for the four-three arrangement, standard ballad unit, of falling triple rhythm and a pretty straight narrative opening: *Go and ask Robin to bring the girls over / to Sweetwater, said my Aunt*; but what follows the semicolon is explication (*and that was why*), delivered with the authority of perfect iambs, and what follows that is the long sweep of pentameter lines:

It was like a dream of ladies sweeping by
The willows, clouds, deep meadowgrass, and the river.

Gorgeous music, this, thrumming between the formal arrangement of the quatrain and the bicameral balance of the sentence, enough to make us overlook narrative confusion: who is Robin? girl or boy? how old are the visitors, girls in line 1 and ladies in line 3? But we're not too uneasy, yet. In the dream of *willows, clouds, grass* we're busy trying to figure out what exactly Sweetwater is, and the temporary satisfaction from *the river* relaxes us a bit. Still, there are those feminine endings (*over, river*), some wistful sadness.

The next stanza, again one sentence, seems to restart the story. *Robin's sisters and my Aunt's lily daughter / Laughed and talked, and tinkled light as wrens*: our same characters, recurring at a point down the time line. Apparently the narrator has done as instructed—"fetched the neighbor girls to play with your cousin" is what we infer—making a kind of garden party to which the speaker is peripheral but enchanted spectator. Because adult? Because male? As in stanza 1, Ransom shifts gears halfway:

If there were a little colony all hens
To go walking by the steep turn of Sweetwater.

If there were—wasn't he there? And which are they really like, wrens or chickens, lilies or tinkling bells? Are these girls playing dress-up? Playing at being women? We begin to revise their age upward. Meanwhile, something ominous creeps into the adjectives (*little colony, steep turn*) and the falling rhythm of the nouns: *ladies, willows, sisters, daughter, colony, Sweetwater*.

Stanza 3 is where narrative must assert itself—we have the scene, we need action, and the third use of *Sweetwater* signals it will be memorable when it comes. Instead: a genial deflection as the moderator steps to the center of the stage, interposing his own shadow between us and the movie screen, his remembering of event between us and event, and hope of narrative resolution goes out of the poem:

> Let them alone, dear Aunt, just for one minute
> Till I go fishing in the dark of my mind:

The earlier split-sentence construction is now rigid, reinforced by the line-end colon; following it, a new verb tense, interrogative syntax, domestic imagery replaced by the legendary and anachronistic, enjambment across stanzas, an absence of feminine rhyme in stanza 4, and a line of fourteen syllables to strain the pentameter. These shifts register—but what? Impending violence, the tone says. Some primitive sacrifice, the central noun says, "virgins" making more precise that cusp between girls and ladies, lilies and hens. Susannah and the Elders, the participial description says (although Susannah was notoriously NOT robed), making the danger of violation cultural as well as personal.

Whatever actually happened, he's going to tell us only the response to it; the other key noun, *scream*, is buried in a prepositional phrase crammed between two big hunks of dependent syntax:

> Myself a child, old suddenly at the scream
> From one of the white throats which it hid among?

In other words, information in the poem's second half is emotive, not discursive, and is rendered musically: change in key, change in tempo—a lyric strategy. Action, imperative in a story, is displaced by shifts in our relation to the scene; the material of the poem, the true subject, is not what happened but what was felt, the protagonist not one of the girls but the narrator. Readers may labor to infer a story all they like; despite characters, setting, and some indelible event offstage, Ransom has managed to foreclose narrative almost entirely.

He certainly could have had it otherwise. If I read the poem correctly as a double initiation, it seems not dissimilar in its subject to "Janet Waking." There's no doubt which poem is more immediately accessible—stories are like that: companionable. But in the purely narrative piece the wry comedy of diction elevated above its subject (*transmogrifying bee* is the famous example) and the syntactical plays doing the same work (*how exceedingly and purply did the knot swell*) also distance the speaker, and the reader, from the poem's emotional center, the child's real grief. Ironic overview and past tense, which have facilitated narrative so wonderfully, narrow the options at closure, as does the reader's aroused need to know WHAT HAPPENED; in order to broaden and complicate the tone, Ransom must try in rhetoric what he was able to embody in the other poem:

> And weeping fast as she had breath
> Janet implored us, "Wake her from her sleep!"
> And would not be instructed in how deep
> Was the forgetful kingdom of death.

Sequential structure, after all, has its own ferocious appetite.

Sequence, subsequent, consequence—the root is "to follow." Narrative can depart from or rearrange chronology but always plays against the presumption of its stability. If lyric structure fixes points on a graph, narrative fills in the line between them, on which to hang discursive information. Flannery O'Connor said, "[I]n a story something has to happen. A perception is not a story." But perception is precisely the lyric poet's gift, and the lyric poem may be, as Charles Olson said, "one perception immediately followed by another." To grasp this difference clearly, look closely at structure in microcosm, which is to say, syntax:

You were younger than last year,
Younger than the day we were married,
Younger than the day we met.

That's narration—expository information about character that also informs event and, indirectly, the narrator.

What are you doing?
To whom are you smiling?
Where are you going?
Will you not answer me?
Answer! Answer!

That's lyric, nondiscursive and music-derived. Nothing is revealed about the "you" except its silence, but the passage instructs us in what to feel—uncomprehending abandonment. Do you hear how regular rhythm functions there, with the persistent end-stopped dimeter, the syntactical repetition, the small variation (*what, to whom, where, will you not*), the echoed word? It's the same triad played in all its inversions. Here's the full text of Eleanor Ross Taylor's ghost story, "Night":

I spent the night in Chastelton.
The splitting damasks hung in belts;
Those faded colors we admired
Forgot themselves in gray.
Light spider-bagged the baseboards, tired.
I climbed up to the children's room.
I knew the way.
Up steps and past a blistered stile
Along that thick oak balustrade
(You like old things? Behold!)

The carved door hung ajar.
I pushed it wide.
The birds flew from their roosts

And disappeared like mice into the sky.
Below, the garden that one time
Held itself clipped urns, hens, cones,
Of evergreen, had turned
A calendar of wastes,
A zodiac of despairs.
There was somebody there.

It was you.
You were a mortal sheen
Flickering from the negative.
You were younger than last year,
Younger than the day we were married,
Younger than the day we met.
What are you doing?
To whom are you smiling?
Where are you going?
Will you not answer me?
Answer! Answer!

Grief has one great wish and an eager imagination. The speaker has a vision, tries to get some answers, grows increasingly agitated—no raven here but a fair substitute in that *mortal sheen / Flickering from the negative*, and an overt narrative structure, space measuring time:

I climbed up to the children's room.
Up steps and past a stile
Along the balustrade.
I pushed the door open.
The birds flew from their roosts.

Straightforward actions rendered in straightforward declarative sentences (what I think of as narrative syntax because driven by subject and action verb). But Taylor is almost always sly. The story line as I compressed it is boring; her poem is not. From the beginning the linguistic energy resides not in the predicates that carry narrative but in the descriptive asides:

> The splitting damasks hung in belts.
> Light spider-bagged the baseboards, tired.
> The birds . . . disappeared like mice into the sky.
> A calendar of wastes, / A zodiac of despairs.

These renderings form the true plot line—or at least a parallel line not chronological but musical, which is to say, plotted along degrees of intensity: crescendo, thickening chords. And how does she render the central narrative action? Without action: *There was somebody there. / It was you.* Then nothing but copulative verbs, shifting into present tense, then future tense as she refuses to report but enacts:

> You were. . . .
> You were. . . .
> What are you doing?
> To whom are you smiling?
> Where are you going?
> Will you not . . . ?

and the final imperative echoing into the white space: *Answer! Answer!*

But Taylor has more complicated and subtle uses for structural subversion, particularly in more recent poems such as "Where Somebody Died":

> The self refuses to appear
>   in this bare place.
> It fears that mute chair
>   and the still window.
> The sunlight scares it.
> There might rise up a sound.
> The door doesn't like to move,
>   and the crow out there

hesitates; he knows
a hole flown into by mistake
would make a bite of him.
What was sits standstill in the chair,
    hangs, stunned, against the dry-eyed light.
Nobody in sight.
Inanimate things, still lifeless.
This room's so empty
    I doubt I'm standing here;
    there can't be room for me
    and total emptiness.
Only some far-off sounds persist.

The brute truck
    over on the interstate.
The flames in the incinerator
    chewing his old vests.

This poem is the very inverse of "Night." Narrative information
is limited to the title and the title's shading of the poem's first
three adjectives (*bare, mute, still*) and last four lines. Unlike the
broad camera angle that opens "Night" and "Sweetwater," we begin here in closeup, with unadorned, undifferentiated *self, chair,
window, door.* Instead of a cast of characters (Robin, girls, aunt)
or even a companion "I"—the neutrality of objects as protagonists; instead of narrative distance afforded by past tense—
present-tense verbs. "Night" opened with description and moved,
by way of simple action, to confrontation. The predicates here
are internal, conditional, intransitive, or simply omitted. Look
at the pivot, where the poem's only two concrete action verbs
(*sits, hangs*) are smothered in verbals and followed by sentence
fragments:

What was sits standstill in the chair,
hangs, stunned, against the dry-eyed light.
Nobody in sight.
Inanimate things, still lifeless.

Where ARE we? Who is telling this? The answer comes almost as an aside, again abstracted, and without any new narrative information:

> This room's so empty
>   I doubt I'm standing here;
>   there can't be room for me
>   and total emptiness.

The function of the lines, I think, is merely to insert the idiomatic "I," a fast glimpse of the recording sensibility. Merely? What an enormous shift in the tonal ground the lines create. Then back to the generalized, "objective," and intransitive—*Only some far-off sounds persist*—and more fragments:

> The brute truck
>   over on the interstate.
> The flames in the incinerator
>   chewing his old vests.

Because these last five nouns are so particular, and because the context has been so generalized (*place, chair, window, door, what was, emptiness, sounds, room* used in both its meanings), the truck, interstate, and incinerator intrude with tremendous violence (enough to suggest this "somebody" might even have been killed on the highway, if our appetite for story is high).

If ever a poem proved Dobyns's point, and mine, this is it: music and feeling amplified within a suggested narrative frame. Think of its cousin, that pure lyric "After great pain a formal feeling comes"—"pure" because the reader is divorced from narrative context, and even narrative speculation, in the very first line: one article or pronoun suppressed, the other indefinite. But what interests Taylor is how the chill and the stupor coexist with the quotidian (sunlight, noisy traffic), just as what interests her is almost always not the fixed moment of before/after, which is the lyric's province, but how before/after, past/present, then/now continually bleed into one another. In "Where Somebody Died" the title creates an expectation for narrative which the predicates and impersonal pronouns deflect, even as they signal duplicity: this speaker only pretends to be omniscient, impersonal; we discover as the poem unfolds, from the personified door and crow, from the blurted first-person pronoun, from the penultimate adjective (*brute truck*) and the final possessive (*his old vests*), a speaker clearly connected emotionally to the *somebody* of the title. The poem is made of the tension between the suppressed particular story—who died, how he died, his significance to the speaker—and the common reactive grief/terror/guilt, which usually seeks resolution in elegy. Narrative serves action, event, passage of time, revelation of character, but nothing happens here, and the poem is in part about that lack—a ghost story in which there is no ghost, in which time doesn't pass (or heal any wounds either). Try rearranging the order of the sentences: no external logic or sequence is violated. But doing so ruins the poem's shape, and its shapeliness, and our participation in its emotional field; ruins the way that establishing self, door, and crow as dramatis personae allows absence to become one too; and ruins the text's unity and sonority, in which loss registers on sensibility. The poem's indelible impact is in its song, the flames *chewing his old vests* as long as the ink stays on the page.

A plot line, then, of sounds, of feeling. In music, one speaks easily of "line"; each note, even repetitions of the same note, must contribute to the phrase, which builds and subsides in volume or pitch or intensity, and each phrase must relate likewise to the others in the overall structure of the piece. "Where Somebody Died" is far from static: there is movement and energy in the phrasing, from the neutral, objectified *self* to the cautious crow; from the passive *There might rise up a sound* through *inanimate things, still lifeless*; from *The door . . .* through the *total emptiness*; from the first set of sentence fragments through the last—and all contribute to the arc stretching from the title through the burning vests.

What carries these progressions, or phrases, into the reader's right brain, bypassing the discursive habit of language, is the texture of repeated sounds, as tightly woven—albeit less regular, less predictable—as Poe's. To analyze Taylor's, we might first locate all the direct repetitions, as graph points: *still, sound*(s), *chair, there, room, stand, empty.* Then find other repetitions: full and half rhyme (*bare / chair / scares / there, window / crow / knows / hole / flown, sunlight / might / rise / like / bite, refuses / mute / move / room, place / hesitates / mistake / flames*), and all the drone notes —all the S sounds, the initial STs, the Ls, Ms, the short *I*. What's left? *Truck.*

Of course, a texture this thickly chorded can't carry a great deal of narrative information with any clarity. And some readers may miss the inexorable momentum of narrative: this happened, and then this happened, and, running parallel, what might have happened—had not the crop been ruined, if the train had come on time. Narrative literature amplifies this aspect of life story, each fork in the road foreclosing options, opening new ones, making our story ours. In Warren's "The Ballad of Billy Potts," we know the stranger is the murderers' son long before they do—if only they had lifted the victim's shirt and seen the birthmark . . . That tension between potential and actual makes a story compelling.

However, as storytellers know, this linearity is only physiologically and retrospectively true: it isn't really "like life," since it isn't how we experience life. Only after crisis do we see, or think we see, how one thing led to another, how circumstance developed out of prior circumstance and choice and event (which is why past tense is so compatible to narrative). And not even physiologically true. We have the bodies of children, then adults. We have parents, then we don't. We live however long, then we're gone.

The relation of the writer to narrative material is always looking back down a one-way street—even if she has to imagine the future to look back from—and the idea of continuity, of chronology as an allegedly stable external referent, is a matter of temperament, faith, and imagination: there must be some good reason why this happened. Which makes narrative, with its allegiance to sequence and continuity, with its illusion of significance and order, as much a manipulation of experience as the lyric's isolation and examination of moments of extreme emotional dilemma.

Presume the classifiers have it right: that the dominant gene in southern poetry is narrative, that we are born to its structure as Noam Chomsky says we are born to syntactical patterns, or that we inherit a taste for it with our cornbread and collard greens, or develop one from long hours with the Old Testament, rocking on the porch with relatives, or walking the stubblefield with a gun on the shoulder, looking for doves. Presume even that the "southern materials"—family, land, the past—require a linear, discursive structure. The danger is that the opposite becomes equally operative: seeing no other structure, we may limit our subjects to those it most naturally serves, or assume significance where there is none, or write the poems already better written, or overprivilege regional idiosyncrasies. A good poem eludes formulas, and the danger in assumptions—for the writers of a region, or an ethnic group, or a gender, or even a period—is their risk of prescription. Corrupted or subverted structure can serve as a useful impediment, a "resisted motion," to borrow Warren's term, the grit provoking the pearl.

In short, if the narratively impaired can learn to tell a story, even the narrative-fostered, narrative-fated southerner can learn NOT to.[1] One might start with a formal arrangement that counters the linear and sequential with juxtaposition: before/after, then/now, if/then, thesis/antithesis. Such dichotomy is the underlying principle of the sonnet, and it is a sonnet plucked from an existing, known, shared story line full of consequence and continuity that I will end with. It is "The Wall," written by Donald Justice, and readers know well the story he alludes to and keeps out of the poem.

> The walls surrounding them they never saw;
> The angels, often. Angels were as common
> As birds or butterflies, but looked more human.

As long as the wings were furled, they felt no awe.
Beasts, too, were friendly. They could find no flaw
In all of Eden: this was the first omen.
The second was the dream which woke the woman.
She dreamed she saw the lion sharpen his claw.
As for the fruit, it had no taste at all.
They had been warned of what was bound to happen.
They had been told of something called the world.
They had been told and told about the wall.
They saw it now; the gate was standing open.
As they advanced, the giant wings unfurled.

How exactly does one avoid narrative? First, since narrative depends on action, suppress action in the predicates with direct negation, copulative verbs, and passive construction. If action is unavoidable, use dependent syntax.

Second, trust economy, and structure the information through the lyric, or musical, devices of juxtaposition and (as here) repetition:

they never saw . . . she saw . . . they saw it now.

That's the protagonists' plot line.

As long as the wings were furled. . . .
. . . the giant wings unfurled.

That's the antagonist, before and after. Two organizing musical phrases.

Third, create a formal and syntactical context that pushes emphasis away from event. For instance, this poem's five exceptions to past tense are all underscored. Two of them (*the walls surrounding, the lion sharpen*) introduce and close the octave. The past perfect of the sestet

They had been warned. . . .
They had been told. . . .
They had been told and told. . . .

is reinforced by syntactical and lexical repetition, the parallel sentences isolated in regular meter, hard end stops, and rhymes, and also by the empty boxcars those syntactical engines pull behind them—*of what was bound to happen, of something called the world, about the wall*—keeping attention focused on the initial independent clauses. Pattern supplants suspense.

Fourth, distract the reader by introducing new detail to counter expected detail (*lion* instead of snake). Meanwhile, deactivate clock and calendar by eliminating all but two moments in time, then make those two moments correspond to the formal arrangement, here a Petrarchan rhyme scheme. What happens to the chief action, the main event, Eve's irreversible error? There and not there, acknowledged and dismissed simultaneously by dependent syntax (*As for the fruit . . .*) and the line's half rhyme with the octave (*claw/all*), wedged between present-tense hungry lion and past-perfect parental warnings.

Was ever material for a poem more narrative than this? Was ever a lyric truer to its music? With the given and the made as nicely balanced as sound and sense, line and sentence, emotion and intellect, "The Wall" keeps the narrative meat under our noses but behind the glass.

I like ending a case for subverted structure with a poem of pure structure; it's a way of subverting the structure of the essay, of keeping on the side of description rather than prescription, and perhaps too of avoiding a new set of assumptions about "southern poetry" that risk oversimplification of it. After all, my argument has been more with the labelers than the practitioners—some of my best friends, some of the poets I most admire, frequently perpetrate narrative, and so, occasionally, do I. The point is, even if you're from the South, you don't HAVE to say how they killed the bat.

Note

1. For additional examples of poems on the cusp, poems alive in the tension of sensibility set against its expression, material against its

shaped arrangement, look at Donald Justice's "Anonymous Drawing," in which he imagines a narrative within the frame of a completed artifact, or Eleanor Ross Taylor's "March 9," where past narrative overwhelms present lyric. Or pair up Charles Wright's "Rural Route," lyric experience rendered as story, and "Blackwater Mountain," autobiographical narrative compressed into epiphanic lyrical moment. Or examine how, in Justice's "First Death," the scrupulous narration runs exactly parallel to the barely acknowledged sequence of central events; or the way Fred Chappell's "My Father Washes His Hands" frames the father's story with the listener's response and commentary to make a third dramatic thing; or how James Dickey confounds the temporal and the linear with a profusion of verb tenses in the lyric "The Heaven of Animals"; or how often in Warren's oeuvre the linear structure is hauled in as a vehicle for meditation, not story.

The Flexible Lyric

These days, when genre seems a relic of simpler times, one would hardly blink at Polonius's oxymoronic blurb— "pastoral-comical, historical-pastoral, tragical-historical, tragical-comical-historical-pastoral." For instance, a recent journal article concludes with this flurry of terms: "His short narrative[s], . . . with their sympathetic focus on human behavior, especially in dramatic situations, combine the power of the story and the emotion of the lyric in a way that is highly compressed and formally beautiful" (Mark Jarman, "Aspects of Robinson").

The work thus praised is the rhymed poetry of E. A. Robinson, proposed in the article as precursor to a poem that is "not a formal lyric" by Chase Twichell and a "poem in prose" by Kate Daniels. But the description might also apply to either of the short pieces I heard in January 1997 by Kevin McIlvoy, who writes novels and short stories, and Karen Brennan, who publishes both fiction and poetry. McIlvoy's was a dramatic monologue with refrain, the profane and darkly comic voice of a piano mover who mocks and then cruelly but not inexplicably takes advantage of his customer. Brennan's, though like McIlvoy's a single scene, contained more action and event—or less: a woman describes where she sits, the flowers and buildings, the decreasing numbers of passersby, her hat blowing into the fountain, the stranger who bicycles up and fishes it out, her walk toward home at dusk, the stranger following ominously on his bike, all of this rendered in dependent syntax and anaphora, each sentence beginning "There is . . ." Absent the page, how could listeners have known that these musical pieces were unlined, were prose? Afterward, when Brennan was congratulated on her "strong new poem," she took alarmed exception: if that wasn't a story, she didn't know what one was; McIlvoy's piece, however. . . .

W. H. Auden said it is "a sheer waste of time to look for a definition of the difference between poetry and prose" (*The Dyer's Hand*). Yet differences between *lyric* and *narrative* seem exactly relevant—if only one could be confident what they are. Brennan's rejoinder WAS confident, accommodating structure rather than form. In her piece each action in sequence closed out the possibilities for succeeding action, and each descriptive detail narrowed the narrative circumstance: a story. McIlvoy's scene-with-piano was established and soon departed from, exaggerated, undermined, as the speaker bullied his sketchy opponents: the piano's owner (often conflated into a plural, a class) and his pathetic dog. Rather than dragging us forward inexorably, as in Brennan's piece, time was held in abeyance during the speaker's sustained outburst. Although there were many characterizing "actions" planted shrewdly throughout, there was only a single consequential one, with the barest of circumstantial motivation, placed close to the end with the same deft efficiency as the couplet in a sonnet.

Carl Dennis concludes a lecture on Horace, Lowell, and Bishop this way: "Genres . . . can be used as tools that poets feel free to adapt to the particular demands of their subject. . . . [O]penness to tradition, far from restricting their freedom, may help [writers] give shape to their concerns and free them from . . . the dominant provincialities of their times" ("Mid-Course Corrections," 1997). Dennis is discussing the shift from public to private within single odes, but his observation has even broader implications, as does his reminder that "the impulse to modify the tradition . . . is built into the tradition itself." This cluster of concerns—genre, tradition, modification—seems exactly pertinent to our current literary moment, when poets, with our book-length poems and "novels-in-verse," and prosers, with their "sudden fiction" and "short shorts," are swapping shovels at the rabbit hole.

But for genres to be useful they need to survive—transcend—any particular set of formal conventions, which the art continually outgrows. Linnaeus provides a model for useful analysis. Willow and pine trees share the same structure but differ in texture and form; spider and crab are alike only in form; a velvet dress and a leopard's back, milkweed fluff and a chick's feathers—these pairings have in common only a certain texture. And just as meaningful scientific classification has come to rest on structure—distinctions among species from which Darwin could trace common ancestry—so too, I maintain, does any useful identification of the lyric.

An argument to that effect, however, requires definition of the elements of a poem based on function rather than substance, without the residue of various New Critical agendas and the conflation of terms that we inherited. That is, it resists Cleanth Brooks and Robert Penn Warren's hierarchy, their preoccupation with form to the exclusion of structure, even as it adjusts the exquisite dialectic of John Crowe Ransom that Brooks and Warren unraveled.

Although the New Criticism was far more fractious than we currently suppose, Ransom's formulations of it were always carefully wrought, nowhere more so than in his last full treatment ("Wanted: An Ontological Critic," 1941). One envies its initial assumption, assuredly dispatched:

> A poem differentiates itself for us, very quickly and convincingly, from a prose discourse. We have examined some important new critics who sense this fact but do not quite offer a decisive version of what the differentia is.

The correct answer for Ransom is neither "moralism" nor "emotionalism" but "the kind of structure exemplified by a poem," which

(a) is not so tight and precise on its logical side as a scientific or technical prose structure generally is, and (b) imports and carries along a great deal of irrelevant or foreign matter which is clearly not structural but even obstructive. This a- and b- formulation is what we inevitably come to if we take the analysis our best critics offer. We sum it up by saying that the poem is a loose logical structure with a good deal of local texture.

Ransom had been first of "our best critics" to offer such a definition; by 1941 he is dispatching the heretics. The left hand holds the "paraphrasable core of logic and situation," establishing poetry as dependable discourse (and his famous irony comes in handy here):

> Hence the rule that the poem never quite abandons the firm thread of its argument. It is not a poem at all without its free poetic "texture," of course; but its "texture" is incidental to its main "structure," which is scientific; so that I should have to concede that the poem is really achieved under the patronage, or perhaps we should say the unwilling auspices, of a scientific discourse. ("Positive and Near-Positive Aesthetics," 1943)

"Of course": the right hand wields poetry's unique ability "to recover the denser and more refractory original world which we know loosely through our perceptions and memories," poetry's "kind of knowledge which is radically or ontologically distinct" from the "reduced, emasculated, and docile versions" of the world which are found in scientific discourses" ("Wanted").

So he will have it both ways—at least science, and more than science—by enacting difference through appropriation:

> The structure proper is the prose of the poem, being a local discourse of almost any kind, and dealing with almost any suitable content. The texture, likewise, seems to be of any real content that may be come upon, provided it is so free, unrestricted, and extended, that it cannot properly get into

> the structure. . . . [I]t is an *order* of content, rather than a
> kind of content, that distinguishes texture from structure,
> and poetry from prose. ("Wanted")

The ontological advantage, then, is located in the "incessant di-
version from the argument which is basic in the poetic medium
itself, and which [is] the poetic 'texture'" ("An Address to Kenneth Burke," 1942), and which has "attached itself technically to
a positive center which it did not destroy" ("Positive," 1943).
Structure provides "enough of a valid or scientific argument to
hold it fairly together . . . with a sort of rough logical rigor," and
the poem goes about its essential business, "everywhere particu-
larizing . . . and densifying itself with content . . . not relevant to
the argument" ("Positive").

As one can see, the elegance of the formula provides only the
two categories, structure and texture, into which to sort the various aspects of the poem. And yet, as he had noted,

> [g]iven an object, and a poet burning to utter himself upon it,
> he must take into account a third item, the form into which
> he must cast his utterance. (If we like, we may call it the *body*
> which he must give to his passion.) It delays and hinders him.
> In the process of "composition" the burning passion is sub-
> mitted to cool and scarcely relevant considerations. (*The
> World's Body*, 1938)

"Delay," "hinder," "scarcely relevant"—sounds to me like his de-
scriptions of texture. But in order to support a true ontological
distinction, he places music under structure, now subdividing
the category for the accommodation:

> The meaning employs the words but the meter employs the
> syllables. There is no point-to-point coordination between the
> development of the semantic structure and that of the pho-
> netic structure. The relation between the two in a poetic
> phrase seems something like the relation between two
> melodies in counterpoint. . . . The semantic structure alone,

like the melody in the treble, may be an aesthetic structure, for it is a logical structure which . . . admits body, or texture, as pure logical structures do not; yet the phonetic structure, which would seem perfectly unrelated to it, is made to combine with it. ("Wanted")

As he addresses how they combine, the two kinds of structure, semantic and phonetic, resemble something like intention and circumstance: the argument "must be partly indeterminate . . . for it is going to be undetermined by the meter. Conversely, a metrical form must be partly indeterminate if it proposes to study an argument." In the interchange that is composition, "the poem is the resultant of two processes interacting upon each other; they come from opposite directions" as the prose discourse is "reduced into the phonetic pattern" or "assimilate[d] to" determinate sound and vice versa ("Wanted").

Nevertheless, he had left the door open while he repaired the lock, and Ransom's discrimination of a variety of structures and textures would be blurred by disciples and heretics alike. In the intervening years between the essays' first proposition and their final refinement, Cleanth Brooks, J. T. Purser, and Robert Penn Warren's influential textbook, *An Approach to Literature*, had appeared (1936), a "natural outgrowth of work in the classroom . . . in courses varying from freshman English . . . to a seminar in Milton"—where its ubiquitous offspring, *Understanding Poetry* (1938), would soon enjoy a long-lived monopoly. Here are three relevant glossary entries, maddeningly tautological, from 1936.

FORM: the arrangement of the various elements in a work of literature; organization of various materials (ideas, images, characters, setting, rhythm, etc.) to give a single effect.

STRUCTURE: Generally speaking, the structure of a work is its total make-up, its form. But there is a tendency to use structure with special reference to the arrangement of episodes, statements, scenes, and details of action as

contrasted with the arrangement of words, for which the
term style is specifically used.

STYLE: Style is in the largest sense the arrangement of
material which the writer makes. More particularly, the
term is used to indicate the arrangement of his words for
expressing special tone, attitude, manner, etc.

Brooks is even more pointed in *The Well Wrought Urn*:

But though it is in terms of structure that we must describe
poetry, the term "structure" is certainly not altogether satis-
factory as a term. One means by it something far more internal than the metrical pattern, say, or than the sequence of
images. The structure meant is certainly not "form" in the
conventional sense in which we think of form as a kind of
envelope which "contains" the "content." . . .

The structure meant is a structure of meanings, evalua-
tions and interpretations; and the principle of unity which
informs it seems to be one of balancing and harmonizing
connotations, attitudes and meanings.

If "form" was barely mentioned by Ransom except as a "code
of manners," a "hindrance to direct action" (*World's Body*), something very much like form was given pride of place by the authors
of the textbooks, which tracked the "concentration and intensification of experience which depends upon an emphasis on the
formal qualities of the poem" (*Approach to Literature*). "Ideal-
ists," Ransom called them, who were "attributing too much virtue to the 'harmonious exercise' in the same poem of imagination
and reason" ("Address"). It's a fairly mild rebuke: in their pages
Ransom's ontological distinction, his stand-off between sound
and meaning, his *free, lively, local, contingent,* and even *irrelevant*
detail was swept away with harmony's broom in the poem's "relatively complex" "pattern of arrangement[,] or the form."

Meanwhile, Brooks's essays were chipping away directly at the
"dualism . . . rarely overcome" introduced by the "heresy of para-

phrase," particularly as practiced by Yvor Winters: "The essential structure of a poem (as distinguished from the rational or logical structure of the 'statement' which we abstract from it) . . . is a pattern of resolved stresses. . . . It is a pattern of resolutions and balances and harmonizations, developed through a temporal scheme (*Well Wrought Urn*).[1]

When Randall Jarrell challenged his elders in a lecture at Princeton in 1942, he conjured a pox on all their houses: he would "disregard the musical structure of poetry: metre, stanza-form, rhyme, alliteration, quantity, and so on" in order to talk about "other sorts of structure in lyrical poetry" and the more important dialectic WITHIN those structures; after all, "unity is not enough."[2] As Auden would soon point out with his usual pith,

> verse is unsuited to controversy, to proving some truth or belief which is not universally accepted. . . .

> Thirty days hath September,
> April, June and November

> is valid because nobody doubts its truth. Were there, however, a party who passionately denied it, the lines would be powerless to convince him because, formally, it would make no difference if the lines ran:

> Thirty days hath September,
> August, May and December. (*The Dyer's Hand*)

How richly the debate might have continued if Jarrell had joined the fray more publicly. But the debate did not continue, nor was the ubiquitous conflation of terms untangled during the intervening fifty years: we learned the method entire and kept that residue when we tossed the method out. Now the preference has resurfaced without the method; primacy of form, still hazily interchangeable with structure, is reasserted with new vigor, this time NOT, as Brooks and Warren had done, excluding a "conventional sense . . . of form as a kind of envelope which 'contains' the 'content.'" To restore any sense of structure as distinct from form, which is my project here, it seems necessary to return to, and update, the paraclete.

In discourse, words perform as semaphore—that is, as Ransom said, they *signify*: "an ethical situation, a passion, a train of thought, a flower or landscape, a thing" ("Criticism as Pure Speculation"). In poems, compression and song will freight the signifiers with additional, usually emotive, information. Compression and song, of course, are the characteristics most firmly assigned to the lyric and they release a poem for "excursions into particularity," its "sense of the real density and contingency of the world in which arguments and plans have to be pursued" ("Criticism"). Hence the torque placed on structure by texture, on the determinate by the indeterminate, on a "paraphrasable core of logic and situation" by a "context of lively local details." Hence in its popularized reduction, the oldest commandment in the creative writing manual: show don't tell.

> [Art] is forever unlike science, in the following respect. The sign which science employs is a mere sign, or "symbol," that is, an object having no other character—for the purpose of discourse at least—than that of referring to another object which is its semantical object. . . . But the aesthetic signs are "icons," or images. As signs they have semantical objects, or refer to objects, but as iconic signs they also resemble or imitate these objects. ("Wanted")

This difference in substance underwrote Ransom's quarrel with Brooks and Warren, and he was adamant that

> [t]he image is one thing, and the rational structure is another thing. The difference between the heterogeneous properties is absolute. Absolute also is the difference between the local imagery of the poem and its logical structure. Their being furnished both comfortably in one poem is a strange coincidence. ("Address")

But all of a poem is "told," one mind speaking to or overheard by another mind, and not so absolute is a corresponding difference in the reader's brain. Neuroscience has been quite busy since the 1940s, and although pathology suggested a strict lateralization (left hemisphere for reason, right for art), newer findings posit a more elaborate circuitry. We know, for instance, that we process very quickly this observation: the flower is dying because of a parasite. A more precise, more sensory noun—a daisy or a rose—triggers other synapses, in other language centers, accessing new information: open-faced, sturdy, plentiful, a weed in a field a bug might crawl across; or a swirl of delicate, fragrant petals, hybrid on the manor grounds, enclosing the worm. But in any sort of discourse the brain's hardware and software are continuously, rapidly parsing the branching syntactical tree—deciding, for instance, that "rose" is a noun and not an adjective or a verb. A poem's rhythms work, in part, to reinforce, to punctuate, a branch at a time, allowing in more of the cultural history of "rose," beyond the empirical memory bank. And there is that heft in the word itself—its one syllable and long vowel extended by the sibilant consonant; in clear syntax this sonic stress can hold us at the fork long enough to retrieve, in what psycholinguists call "breadth-first search," the flash of a woman's name or a medieval lay or the Rose of Sharon before the sentence presses us into the "depth-first search" that "gambles . . . about the alternative most likely to be true."[3] And there is, for a poem, the occasion of the utterance as well. Brooks would be right to contrast my bland paraphrase with Blake's opening line, "O Rose, thou art sick," which supplies—in its formality of diction and syntax, in its choice of pronoun, in its relationship of stressed and unstressed syllables, in its dance of long vowels and hard final consonant—access to the sensory and cultural information latent in the concrete noun, to the attitude in the observation (that is, tone), and to something very like a kinetic response to pitch and timbre, tempo and inflection.[4]

But ALL OF THIS contributes to the texture of the line. The hardest aspect to translate from another language, texture is the easiest to alter in one's own; most revision consists of such adjustments, which then open some newly visible patterns or another and more effective organization. Blake's rose, worm, and sexual storm do make a network of their associations, but that is less an "argument" than the web the bird sees, flying over; meanwhile, texture puts us inside it, synapses firing. To a large extent, it is the poem strand by strand—not the "context" but the text itself as it is apprehended.

Thus, it is the testy polarity of Ransom's "loose logical structure" and "irrelevant local texture" ("absolute . . . is the difference") that I'd like to complicate and realign, proposing analysis by function rather than substance. Doing so maintains texture as a poem's silk or oak or clay—common to both structure and form, which can nonetheless be differentiated (*pace* Brooks and Warren)—and leaves joined, as they are in successful poems, the logical and the local, the paraphrasable and the ineffable. With such an approach the productive inquiry becomes whether, in the completed work, any particular wooden wall is weight-bearing, or put there for the elegance of design.

To say a building has a sound structure means that the foundation and frame are adequate for the shape and weight; barns stand up under heavy snow because there are enough beams spaced close enough together—their relation is less logical than pragmatic. By extension, structure in poems seems neither "paraphrasable" content (idea, observation, perception), which Ransom saw as complexly—under "metric compulsion"—"compounded" in image, figure, diction, and tone; nor Brooks's "achieved harmony," clearly "distinguished from the rational or logical statement"; but rather the support for both content and its embodiment in the words chosen and arranged in harmony or tension. That is, structure is the way all the poem's materials are organized, whether they are abstract or concrete, precise or suggestive, denoted or connoted, sensory or referential, singular or recurring. Since almost all poems in English are linear—read left to right and down the page—structure is also the purposeful order in which materials are released to the reader, whereas form creates pattern in these materials, to establish pleasing proportion, balance, unity—"a single effect"—in an otherwise over-whelmingly various texture.

A list, for instance, is not only a crude form but a pure one: its sole function is to include and exclude. A shopping list, recorded chronologically, has an order of sorts, one item following another, but lacks pragmatic structure unless reordered and organized: fresh vegetables and fruits listed first, then meats, then dairy, to reflect the layout at the Piggly-Wiggly. If, on the other hand, in revision the list is merely alphabetized, the imposed arrangement is artifice, strictly formal; the accidental "arrangement" has been replaced by a systematic one, but the list remains without any necessary progression or subordination, any FUNC-TIONAL structure. It is just such pure and democratizing unity that makes one list outrageous—

> make dinner
> walk the dog
> go to town
> shoot my mother
> buy a blouse
> watch TV

—and another one shrewd: "Puffs, powders, patches, Bibles, billets-doux."

By contrast, syntax in our uninflectional language makes meaning precisely through sequence and lexical relationships; it is a structure. With almost any extended syntax, progression and subordination are inherent and can contribute to a list an inevitable and informative source of organization, even while syntactical rhythms are being managed to create pattern and "single effect." Here are "those who came to Gatsby's house that summer":

> the Chester Beckers and the Leeches, and a man named
> Bunsen, whom I knew at Yale, and Doctor Webster Civet, who
> was drowned last summer up in Maine. And the Hornbeams
> and the Willie Voltaires, and a whole clan named Blackbuck,

who always gathered in a corner and flipped up their noses
like goats at whosoever came near. And the Ismays and the
Chrysties (or rather Hubert Auerbach and Mr. Chrystie's
wife), and Edgar Beaver, whose hair, they say, turned cotton-
white one winter afternoon for no good reason at all.

The names cited last are not necessarily funnier than the first;
they are all entries on the grocery list. Our delight comes from
Fitzgerald's arc, a shapeliness supplied by repetition of the equal-
izing conjunction and by the trailing subordinate clauses of increasing length:

whom I knew at Yale
who was drowned last summer up in Maine
who always gathered in a corner and flipped up their noses
    like goats at whosoever came near
whose hair, they say, turned cotton-white one winter
    afternoon for no good reason at all

What accrues—what is structured—is increasing boldness in
the commentary *on* the list, a darkening of tone, and thereby a
purposeful movement through the allusions, assonance, alliteration, anaphora, phrasal repetition and rhyme (*a man named Bun-
sen, a clan named Blackbuck*), images, figuration, puns, varying
levels of diction, and onomatopoeia.

In most poems, to these same elements of linguistic texture is
added lineation, which provides both an additional rhythmic system and additional opportunities to make discernible pattern,
which in turn may seem to "give a single effect." Pattern alone,
however, does not account for powerful structure, any more than
repeated nouns or phrases in a list. As Jarrell reminds us,

The sort of unity that is generated by mere homogeneity or
similarity is plainly insufficient for poetry. A . . . monotonous
series has a high degree of unity, of the wrong sort[;] . . . the
organization of a good poem, so full of strain and tension, is
obtained not merely by intensifying the forces working toward

a simple unity, but by intensifying the opposing forces as well. ("Levels and Opposites")

Gilbert Murray, writing on Greek and Latin meter, makes a similar point about "internal structure—as distinguished from a repeated pattern":

> In elegiac verse, the unit is a couplet; and the couplet not only consists of two lines divided into symmetrical halves— that is symmetry: it also ends on a rhythm which would be uninteresting to the ear unless it were led up to by a series of rhythms which do not receive their full explanation until it comes—that is architecture. (*The Classical Tradition in Poetry*)

If we can distinguish as "form" the arrangement of texture in a poem to create pattern, recurrence, symmetry, harmony, and unity; and as "structure" the organization, the architecture, "so full of strain and tension," of a poem's textural materials; then perhaps we can end the residual conflation of terms and the current suspicion that a poem can succeed with one and not the other.

II

The important test cases would be those compressed lyrics that appear to have alchemized the distinct elements past differentiation. Here's one:

> With how sad steps, Oh Moon, thou climb'st the skies,
> How silently, and with how wan a face!
> What, may it be that even in heav'nly place
> That busy archer his sharp arrows tries?
> Sure, if that long-with-love-acquainted eyes
> Can judge of love, thou feel'st a lover's case;
> I read it in thy looks: thy languished grace,
> To me that feel the like, thy state descries.

Then even of fellowship, Oh Moon, tell me,
Is constant love deemed there but want of wit?
Are beauties there as proud as here they be?
Do they above love to be loved, and yet
Those lovers scorn whom that love doth possess?
Do they call virtue there ungratefulness?
   (Philip Sidney, Sonnet 31, from *Astrophel and Stella*;
   composed c. 1580, first known publication 1591)

The Petrarchan sonnet may have endured in large part because of the built-in satisfactions of its rhyme scheme: the octave's matched, interlocked quatrains (*abbaabba*), then the sestet's looser deployment of three new end sounds over six lines
(*cdecde* in the paradigm). That eight-six pattern is often reinforced by the syntax and punctuation, providing the rhymes increased duration. It is reinforced here as well by clustered consonants (*S* sounds in lines 1 and 4, *L*s in 5–8) and midline use
of the vowels from the octave's end rhymes, *I* and *A* (*climb'st,
silently, may, acquainted, thy, they, like, thy state*). Like inversions
of the tonic chord in a sonata's exposition, these textural repetitions further unify, and distinguish, the first eight lines: that long
I never appears in the sestet, the long *A* just once (in the poem's
last word—*ungratefulness*).

What yokes the distinct sections of the poem? Regular meter
(iambic pentameter) and, in Sidney's "With how sad steps," also
a high degree of sustained repetition, even among unstressed
monosyllabic words not crucial to the argument. *Thy* appears
three times in two lines, replicates an end-rhymed vowel, and al-
literates with *that* (five times), *there* (three times), *they* (three
times), *thou* (twice), *then*, and *those*; only one line in the poem
lacks this alliteration, and that is line 2, which has its own repetition, its own references to the surrounding lines. Likewise, *love*
occurs in lines 5, 6, 10, 12, and 13, *lovers* in 6 and 13, and *loved* in
12, meanwhile alliterated with *long, looks, languished,* and *like.*
Indeed, twelve of the poem's fourteen lines contain at least one
use of *L*, often in combination with rhyming sounds in the same

or adjacent lines. In short, an interior, overarching, and opportunistic textural pattern links the eight-six rhymed blocks to create a highly unified musical field, "a single effect." This formal
patterning—this music—may contribute to tone and thereby
to content, but it does not necessarily have any organizational
(structural) function.

By *opportunistic* I mean that sense of play and discovery which
Ransom accommodated as "indeterminate," designated here as
texture managed to create pattern, and consequently form not restricted to meter or rhyme scheme. An example of opportunistic
formal brilliance may be seen in the two Sidney lines that do NOT
include the L. The first is line 4, which he has slowed by intensifying the other dominant consonant (which appears in thirteen
lines): five S sounds in ten syllables. There is also energetic alternation of short and long vowels in conjunction with meter,
stutter-steps preparatory to a leap: that BIZ-ee AH-cher HIZ SHAHP
A-roze TRIZE.

But this is not only effective pattern and variation WITHIN the
line; Murray's "construction" is at work in meter made "more emphatic to the ear" by end rhyme. That is, the unbroken pentameter resolves the interruptions and hesitations that preceded it:

> With how sad steps//Oh Moon//thou climb'st the skies,
> How silently//and with how wan a face!
> What//may it be that even in heav'nly place
> That busy archer his sharp arrows tries?

As in the Greek and Latin verse Murray analyzes, the passage

> divides into four; and each member is an attempt, and a dif-
> ferent attempt, at the rhythm which is at last perfected in
> the fourth member . . . to which all three [others] lead by
> a kind of progress. The last . . . is extraordinarily delight-
> ful in rhythm; but it would be nothing in particular if it
> were not reached by a struggle—and just the right kind
> of struggle. [This is] not mere repetition of a pattern; [it is]
> a constructed whole.

Within this architecture, pattern and variation are not merely decorative; the formal resolution completes the first quatrain's invocation and presumption and thereby corresponds to the resolution of the first movement of the thought, the first postulate of the poem's argument.

The same functional contribution of formal arrangement can be observed in Sidney's other *L*-deprived line: *Are beauties there as proud as here they be?* As usual, his elaborate ear is at work, with the alliterative *there . . . they* and *beauties . . . be*, the half-rhyme progression of *Are . . . there . . . here*, the unstressed long *E* (*bu-teez*) preparatory to its end-stopped masculine rhyme. But what cements the line, beyond metrical regularity, is chiasmus (which Shakespeare will appropriate as one of his stylistic signatures): within the two forms of the verb which anchor the ends of the line-long sentence (*Are . . . be*) and the interior frame of noun and its referent (*beauties . . . they*), one finds this wonderfully balanced center: *there as proud as here*. In other words, the sentence spins down into the central accusation and then back out pretty much in its own footsteps, providing the line enormous integrity and independence.

Again, placement of this line is not arbitrary: unlike the octave's syntactically closed couplets it is the first of two line-long, freestanding interrogatives, one here, one at the end. In other words, Sidney uses formally reinforced syntactical rhythms, rather than end rhyme, to subdivide the sestet exactly as the strict Italian rhyme scheme does (*cde cde*)—into units of three set against the octave's interlocking couplets—even as the end rhymes provide a departure (*cdcdee*).

So great is our love of pattern, of formal pleasures, that this kind of departure from the Petrarchan model was long considered a flaw, a vulgarity passed along by Thomas Wyatt, contracted perhaps from the work of minor poets abroad.[5] But form in a memorable poem is never passive, never simply a concrete mold into which the intermingling materials of the poem are poured (nor in free verse an accidental byproduct of the sweaty tussles of detail and idea). A rhyme scheme is only one formal tool at the poet's disposal, and not the chief one. Although un-conventional, Sidney's sestet is formally impeccable, the *-ell* rhymes of line 9 settling briefly into *love* in line 10, disappearing to isolate the freestanding sentence of line 11, then reemerging in the two-line sentence that follows (*love . . . loved . . . / lovers . . . love*) to make chime the buried rhyme in line 14 (*call . . . un-gratefulness*), which reverses the pair that opened the sestet (*fel-lowship . . . tell*). Meanwhile, we are borne steadily toward clo-sure by the continuo S, softened and medial in lines 9 and 10 (*fellowship, constant*), unstressed in line 11, missing altogether in line 12, then erupting in line 13 to prepare for the rhymed stressed hiss that ends the poem (*ungratefulness*).

The traditional sonnet, of course, links the binary rhyme scheme to argument and paradox. In the Petrarchan arrange-ment the interlocked octave and the distinct sestet delineate, by convention, a situation and its implications, a question and its answer, doubt followed by comfort, experience and then mean-ing, or past difficulty and present resolution: the fixed formal arrangement is duplicated by, or duplicates, the structure. In such a case form's function seems incontrovertible: after the yoked quatrains (*abbaabba*) complete initial exposition, the poem employs a *volta*, or turn, to swing into the second half of the utterance, presenting simultaneously a contradiction of what has preceded and a natural fulfillment of it, with new rhyming sounds (*c d e*) in a new, looser pattern. Meanwhile, the slight asymmetry (six formally open lines balancing eight formally con-stricted lines) draws us into resolution and closure.

Thus it is in Sidney's #31. Once the moon's potential for empa-thy is established, there is more than a shift in end sounds, or a rhetorical signal, at line 9; the turn is articulated musically in the patterns made by recurring consonants or long vowels, allit-erated or fully repeated words, and syntactical arrangements. At the same time, the end rhyme, one of his two most noticeable for-mal patterns (the other being meter), is coincident with structure in the octave, oppositional to structure in the sestet.

"Oppositional," of course, reveals expectations for the paradigm. In biology the function of both exo- and endoskeletons is to support the organs. An exoskeleton can take many forms, turtle shell or locust husk, but is always visible and directly corresponds to form; the endoskeleton supports from within, whether the external shape is human or horse or whale. Likewise, we assume that in conventional "fixed" forms—the rhymed sonnet, the ghazal, the haiku—structure will be exoskeletal and coincident with form, that in free verse or open-form poems it will be submerged. But this need not be—has not forever been—the case, as Sidney's sestet demonstrates. Perhaps only the intervening centuries of genre definition based on form—in particular a notion of form which aspires, in its direct coincidence with structure, to Platonic ideal—supplied the imperative.

Meanwhile, I'd like to track a second exoskeletal paradigm, texture again directed simultaneously toward form and structure:

> That time of year thou mayst in me behold
> When yellow leaves, or none, or few, do hang
> Upon those boughs which shake against the cold,
> Bare ruined choirs where late the sweet birds sang.
> In me thou see'st the twilight of such day
> As after sunset fadeth in the west;
> Which by and by black night doth take away,
> Death's second self, that seals up all in rest.
> In me thou see'st the glowing of such fire,
> That on the ashes of his youth doth lie,
> As the deathbed whereon it must expire,
> Consumed with that which it was nourished by.
> This thou perceiv'st, which makes thy love more strong,
> To love that well which thou must leave ere long.
>
>   (William Shakespeare, Sonnet 73;
>   sequence composed c. 1592–96)

Again the presiding spirit is *logos*, the important relation is paradox; again form and structure are coincident. Where this paradigm most substantially differs from the Italian is in the placement of the *volta*—now at line 12—and the concomitant rhyme scheme. As in the Fitzgerald paragraph, the first twelve lines of Sonnet 73 offer a single perception, as though citing relevant legal precedents to a judge; nothing actually develops except the persuasive power of the accumulating examples. In addition to the pentametric glue the lines are formally grouped by end rhyme, the three end-stopped, syntactically complete quatrains given simultaneous independence and connection by the parallel rhyme scheme (*abab cdcd efef*): independence in the end sounds, connection in their pattern. Additional marshaling of texture can be tracked in the parallel metaphors, one per quatrain—winter coming, night falling, fire dying—images of repletion to illustrate what "In me thou see'st," and each deployed in its own four-line sentence.

That these three quatrains couldn't get much more alike increases the power of the startling asymmetry—an elephant balanced on a footstool—created by the variation, a closed couplet to replace the leisurely lope of alternating rhyme and to introduce new end sounds (*gg*):

This thou perceiv'st, which makes thy love more strong,
To love that well which thou must leave ere long.

In other words, a shift in rhyme pattern replicates the structural shift or turn in the argument—a turn not logical but dramatic. The couplet's first clause restates the quatrains' repeated assertion in the same syntax (object first) of the poem's opening line; its last clause makes explicit the three extended metaphors. Between them the paradox is embedded—*which makes thy love more strong / To love that well*—to devastate the prosecution's case.

So much for repeated pattern. There is also architecture here, and the poem's structure comprises more than just a twelve-line list followed by negation; its series of metaphors is carefully ordered, in the sort of sequence W. K. Wimsatt called a "qualitative progression" of images. If we disturb the order, reversing, say, the second and third quatrains to insert the fire between images of calendar and clock, no harm is done to the rhyme scheme; and we could tolerate other formal damage, such as the loss of the satisfying movement in the end-rhymed long vowels from closed to open, from *O* (first quatrain) to *A* (second) to *I* (third)—the last extended with slant rhyme to the alternating pair (*fire/lie/expire/by*)—before they are replaced altogether (*long/strong*). Intolerably lost, however, would be the effective structure, the intensity and focus of the original: seasons mark a year, sunset ends a day, a fire dies out in even less time, the twelve lines gathering momentum toward their own paradoxical closure, "Consumed with that which it was nourished by." And that same movement collects, as it goes, increased desperation—the seasons and days are renewable, the fire that is one's life is not—adding force to the codicil: unlike the examples cited, frailty of its object makes love stronger.

The structure, then, is what secures a functional contribution from each textural pleasure, each formal pattern. Leafless boughs shake, sunset fades into black, a fire goes out—this sequence, even lacking narrative consequence, is crucial to the poem's "felt thought" (Eliot's term), sweeping us toward death irrevocable and then revoked. To appreciate its authority, we need only compare this couplet to that which closed Sidney's Sonnet 31.

In both sonnets, with their distinct determinate formal patterns and equally distinct structures, such thorough concurrence of structure and form—a spider's web—achieves a quite particular ideal, one consonant with, let's say, a strict hierarchy running upward from pebbles to Paradise, one in which the folly of a king disturbs the weather. Conversely, in that world view, balanced exterior forms signal internal order, a "right" arrangement deep in the structure of the world. Lacking these broad assumptions, strictly aesthetic residue can be both poignant and superficial; more detrimentally, form overtly aligned with artifice is sometimes disguised as, or meant to supplant, structure. And herein lies my resistance to some of the current fierceness about formal conventions of meter and rhyme without too much fussing over their function.

To return to an earlier observation: every English poem is linear, read (or heard) left to right, top to bottom, and similarly processed. Narrative knows this and works openly or slyly in the discursive or linear grain, tracking possibility and consequence, which in turn depend on some assumption of time-driven sequence. Like trauma, lyric contradicts the linear—it "stops time" —and to do so uses simultaneous, sometimes opposing perceptions, a dense fabric of emotive language, highly musical arrangements of texture, and alternative organizations of those arrangements. The structures codified by Petrarch and Shakespeare were just such alternatives, devised in general service to lyric and particular service to paradox. Meanwhile, certainly in the case of our English paragon—who blatantly inserted sonnets into plays, dramatic monologue and soliloquy and narrative sequence into sonnets—form seems not to have been privileged over structure, as is the current predisposition, but rather to have been, as Stevens puts it, what would suffice.[6]

It's important to recall the long search, in the two hundred years following Petrarch (1304–1374), for ways to adapt the magnificent Italian arrangement to other languages. The French solution was alexandrines, and Sidney and Spenser also tried hexameter, but the major impediment for English, an uninflected and opportunistic language of multiple lexical derivation, was the difficulty of finding such frequent natural rhyme. In two translations of the same poem by Petrarch—both manuscripts dated 1557, both preserving the clear *volta*, the bivalve structure of the original—one can see Wyatt and the Earl of Surrey each striking his own compromise.[7] Wyatt observes convention in the octave's rhymes but forgoes strict meter and takes liberties in the sestet (*cdccdd*). Surrey keeps pentameter but does so in the looser alternating rhyme of the ballad stanza.

The very real problem with alternating rhyme is in the arithmetic: you can't divide fourteen by four without two lines left over. By 1580 and the first sonnet cycle in English (Sidney's *Astrophel and Stella*, modeled on Petrarch's *Canzoniere* and Dante's *Vita Nuova*), the "Englished" sestet used by Surrey was well established: three new sounds arrayed in a ballad quatrain and more or less disguised couplet, Italian form internalized with syntax and enjambment:

> But words came halting forth, wanting Invention's stay;
> Invention, Nature's child, fled stepdame Study's blows;
> And others' feet still seemed but strangers in my way.
> Thus, great with child to speak, and helpless in my throes,
> Biting my truant pen, beating myself for spite:
> "Fool," said my Muse to me, "look in thy heart, and write."
>   (Sidney, Sonnet 1)

> If that be sin which doth the manners frame,
> Well stayed with truth in word and faith of deed,
> Ready of wit, and fearing naught but shame;
> If that be sin which in fixed hearts doth breed
> A loathing of all loose unchastity,
> Then love is sin, and let me sinful be.
>   (Sidney, Sonnet 14)

"Englished," that is, in the end rhymes, not in the structure. The poems still employed a Petrarchan octave, strictly rhymed (*abbaabba*) or with alternating but REPEATED rhyme (*abababab*); the octave-sestet division, and the powerful way it could leverage argument, was sacrosanct.

As far as we know, Shakespeare was never so wed to received paradigm. By the 1590s (earliest consensus date for the sonnets) he had developed enormous formal facility—sustaining couplets at will[8]—in the set pieces lodged within the plays completed, performed, or at least under way: *Comedy of Errors, Love's Labour's Lost, Romeo and Juliet, Two Gentlemen of Verona,* all of

*Henry VI, Richard III, The Taming of the Shrew, A Midsummer
Night's Dream*. It isn't much of a stretch to suppose that as the
plays moved away from rhyme into blank verse, the ballad's accommodation of English speech (and perhaps its low-culture
popularity) encouraged his immediate employment of full alternating rhyme for the sonnet sequence.

But neither does genius reinvent the wheel. Three early sonnets will illustrate.[9]

> When I do count the clock that tells the time,
> And see the brave day sunk in hideous night;
> When I behold the violet past prime,
> And sable curls all silver'd o'er with white;
> When lofty trees I see barren of leaves
> Which erst from heat did canopy the herd,
> And summer's green all girded up in sheaves
> Borne on the bier with white and bristly beard,
> Then of thy beauty do I question make,
> That thou among the wastes of time must go,
> Since sweets and beauties do themselves forsake
> And die as fast as they see others grow;
> And nothing 'gainst Time's scythe can make defence
> Save breed, to brave him when he takes thee hence.
>
>   (Shakespeare, Sonnet 12)

> Shall I compare thee to a summer's day?
> Thou art more lovely and more temperate:
> Rough winds do shake the darling buds of May,
> And summer's lease hath all too short a date:
> Sometimes too hot the eye of heaven shines,
> And often is his gold complexion dimm'd;
> And every fair from fair sometime declines,
> By chance of nature's changing course untrimm'd;
> But thy eternal summer shall not fade
> Nor lose possession of that fair thou owest;

Nor shall Death brag thou wander'st in his shade,
When in eternal lines to time thou growest:
So long as men can breathe or eyes can see,
So long lives this and this gives life to thee.

(Shakespeare, Sonnet 18)

When, in disgrace with fortune and men's eyes,
I all alone beweep my outcast state
And trouble deaf heaven with my bootless cries
And look upon myself and curse my fate,
Wishing me like to one more rich in hope,
Featured like him, like him with friends possess'd,
Desiring this man's art and that man's scope,
With what I most enjoy contented least;
Yet in these thoughts myself almost despising,
Haply I think on thee, and then my state,
Like to the lark at break of day arising
From sullen earth, sings hymns at heaven's gate;
For thy sweet love remember'd such wealth brings
That then I scorn to change my state with kings.

(Shakespeare, Sonnet 29)

As in all the alleged first twenty-nine sonnets and some of the later numbers, the eight-six structure is firmly in place in these three, complete with announced rhetorical signal at the *volta*. But one can see in the trajectory of this sample how the rhymed couplet, never disguised by syntax as Sidney's and Surrey's had been, becomes more and more a structural opportunity. In #12, it's only a logical extension of the turn at lines 9–10:

thou among the wastes of time must go, . . .
And nothing 'gainst Time's scythe can make defence
Save breed, to brave him when he takes thee hence.

In #18, repetition and end-stopped rhymes call attention to a new resolve, a shift in tone, rhyme, and the introduction of one of the sequence's great themes:

> But thy eternal summer shall not fade . . .
> So long as men can breathe or eyes can see,
> So long lives this and this gives life to thee.

By #29, as the syntax unscrolls his most seamless octave yet, we find signals of something seismic at some new distance from the old fault line, as the continental plates of paradox push against each other. If in lines 9–12 the speaker can suddenly, luckily, be distracted from his misery—*like to the lark . . . arising / From sullen earth*—in the last two lines the penury itself (*disgrace with fortune*) is outright overturned (*such wealth brings*).

What has emerged is a distinct second *volta*. In the presumed earlier sonnets the octave establishes the given, the circumstantial, in a series of concrete examples (the violet, trees, and grain; or the winds, the buds, the "gold complexion" of the sun); in the sestet the condition is either enlarged (#12) or diminished (#18) with generality and statement. "When, in disgrace . . ." suggests the same strategy, as he makes the turn at line 9 with what seems a straightforward summary and recapitulation (*Yet in these thoughts myself almost despising*). But there is also a submerged sequence, or progression, at work in the three quatrains, one that links, in a clearly chiasmic logic, *deaf heaven . . . cries* (line 3) to *hymns . . . heaven's gate* (line 12) and is carefully parsed out in the verbs and verbals in between: *beweep, trouble, look, curse, wishing, desiring, despising, think, sings*. Only in the couplet, with the poem's final, dramatic predicate action (*I scorn to change my state with kings*), does he redirect the invidious comparisons.

The pattern of verbs and verbals is also doing some formal work, aligning the first and third quatrains with independent predicates (*I beweep . . . and trouble . . . and look . . . and curse; I think . . . and my state . . . sings hymns*), while consigning the second quatrain to participles (*wishing, featured, possess'd, desiring, contented*), which will reappear, rhymed, in the third as well (*despising, arising*). And there's another "qualitative progression" or architecture in the meter, from the reversed initial foot that opens the poem (WHEN, in disGRACE) to its repetition in the second quatrain (WISHing me LIKE; FEAtured like HIM), to the tripled use in the third (YET in these THOUGHTS; HAPly I THINK; LIKE to the LARK). Similarly, instead of distracting from the tag rhyme of the couplet with triadic syntax in lines 9–14, as Wyatt, Surrey, and Sidney had done, Shakespeare reinforces it: those three initial trochees build toward the poem's one enjambment, spilling us past Sidney's old resting place at line 11, the Italian sestet's midpoint (*cde cde*), and into a new one at the end of line 12, created by the delayed predicate and final close alliteration:

> Yet in these thoughts myself almost despising,
> Haply I think on thee, and then my state,
> Like to the lark at break of day arising
> From sullen earth, sings hymns at heaven's gate. . . .

This is a management of texture allied with the English rhyme scheme, not the older Italian, and stitching all three quatrains into a unit of considerable formal integrity. Meanwhile, rhetorical signals are left to free-float and duplicate, the usual "when, yet" waving the Petrarchan flag but with additional flags—*then, then*—late in line 10 and early in line 14.

This evolution toward the English paradigm strikes me as greatly suggestive of Ransom's determinate/indeterminate interchange writ large, since the structural experimentation corresponds with more and more frequent instances of Shakespeare's textural fingerprints, or style. Increasingly in the first twenty-nine sonnets one sees examples of chiasmus and balance, direct or only slightly modified lexical repetition, elaborate sonic architecture, and clustered stresses. Much of this is also period style—Shakespeare, like Mozart, commanded a peerless formal facility—and the second quatrain of #29,

> Wishing me like to one more rich in hope,
> Featured like him, like him with friends possess'd,
> Desiring this man's art and that man's scope,
> With what I most enjoy contented least . . .

recalls Sidney's close repetition, Sidney's balance (*With how sad steps . . . with how wan a face*) and chiasmus (*Are beauties there as proud as here they be*). But the chiasmic syntax in line 6—participles initiating one phrase, concluding the next, exact repetition in the middle—also contains an *abba* arrangement of alliteration in the stressed syllables: *Featured . . . him . . . him . . . friends*. And in lines 11–12, extending pressure from the initial trochees toward the enjambment as the alliterative *think . . . then* echoes *these thoughts* from the previous line, and the hard *K* planted in *think* is elaborated in *Like . . . lark . . . break*, there is Shakespeare's characteristic crescendo of stressed long vowels:

> Yet in these thoughts myself aLMOST desPISING,
> Haply I think on THEE, and then my STATE,
> LIKE to the LARK at BREAK of DAY aRIsing
> From sullen earth . . .

We can also note the emergence of a "Shakespearean" pattern of clustered stresses, no longer simply scattered throughout (*brave day, past prime, Time's scythe, Save breed* in #12; *Rough winds, Death brag* in #18; *deaf heaven, sings hymns* in #29). Now he arranges balanced groups within a single line—

> For THY SWEET LOVE   remember'd   SUCH WEALTH
>   BRINGS (#29)

—sometimes underlined with other repetitions:

> So LONG LIVES THIS   and THIS GIVES LIFE (#18);
> THIS MAN'S ART   and THAT MAN'S SCOPE (#29).

A mere coincidence of textural, formal, and structural authority seems unlikely, especially given their stunning convergence in Sonnet 30:

> When to the sessions of sweet silent thought
> I summon up remembrance of things past,
> I sigh the lack of many a thing I sought,
> And with old woes new wail my dear time's waste;

Then can I drown an eye, unused to flow,
For precious friends hid in death's dateless night,
And weep afresh love's long since cancell'd woe,
And moan the expense of many a vanish'd sight:
Then can I grieve at grievances foregone,
And heavily from woe to woe tell o'er
The sad account of fore-bemoanèd moan,
Which I new pay as if not paid before.
But if the while I think on thee, dear friend,
All losses are restored and sorrows end.

Presumably this one, like #73 ("That time of year . . ."), would be exempt from Ransom's judgment that Shakespeare's sonnets "are generally ill-constructed": "They use the common English metrical pattern, and the metrical work is always admirable, but the logical pattern more often than not fails to fit it" (*World's Body*). It has all the characteristic alliteration, long vowels, direct repetition, clustered stresses, rhythmically and rhetorically balanced lines that mark Shakespearean style:

And WITH OLD WOES NEW WAIL my DEAR TIME'S WASTE; . . .
Which I NEW PAY as IF NOT PAID beFORE.

But now many of those same textural patterns are at work re-aligning structure. Syntax is the most noticeable of these, used by now not only characteristically but also to create structural affinities, paced waves of information. The three rhymed quatrains open with the same metrical variation:

WHEN to the sessions . . .
THEN can I drown . . .
THEN can I grieve . . .

The second and third are linked further, across the old eight-six divide, by direct lexical repetition. And other links are forged among quatrains with close repetition of the long O (in lines 4–5, 7–8, 10–11) and the delayed echoes in lines 3–12 (*I sigh the lack of many . . . many a vanish'd sight*; *a thing I sought . . . a van-*

ish'd sight; old woes . . . cancell'd woe . . . from woe to woe; new wail . . . new pay; foregone . . . fore-bemoanèd . . . before).

The framing lines, which share a more removed tone, seem pretty straightforward in comparison:

> When to the sessions of sweet silent thought
> I summon up remembrance of things past, . . .
> . . . if the while I think on thee, dear friend,
> All losses are restored and sorrows end.

They are the entire argument. Those wandering rhetorical cues of #29 are indeed now set firmly, predictably, at the start of each quatrain (a formal gesture, which will disappear when, as in #73, syntax and repetition do the structural job alone). Nevertheless, lines 3–12 are driven not by *logos* or argumentation so much as by lyric cry: the speaker will *sigh the lack, new wail, drown an eye, weep afresh, moan, grieve at grievances, tell o'er / The sad account,* and *new pay.* As with the images of #73 ("That time of year . . ."), there is, in the long unwinding sentence, a progression here— one of increasing despair, each action an intensification of the same circumstance. Nothing changes until line 13, where everything changes: losses restored, sorrows ended—putting an end as well to Italian structural monopoly.

Darwinist Stephen Jay Gould proposed the term "punctuated equilibrium" to account, in species evolution, for just such sudden radical change after unremarkable eons. My own speculation on a bridge between #29 and #30, the move from eight-six to twelve-two construction, supports this candidate:

> ROM. If I profane with my unworthiest hand
>   This holy shrine, the gentle fine is this:
>   My lips, two blushing pilgrims, ready stand
>   To smooth that rough touch with a tender kiss.
> JUL. Good pilgrim, you do wrong your hand too much,
>   Which mannerly devotion shows in this;
>   For saints have hands that pilgrims' hands do touch,
>   And palm to palm is holy palmers' kiss.

ROM. Have not saints lips, and holy palmers too?
JUL. Ay, pilgrim, lips that they must use in prayer.
ROM. O, then, dear saint, let lips do what hands do;
    They pray, grant thou, lest faith turn to despair.
JUL. Saints do not move, though grant for prayers' sake.
ROM. Then move not, while my prayer's effect I take.
                    (First quarto, 1597; probably composed c. 1591)

Sonnet 30 ("When to the sessions . . .") is, after all, the most dramatic of the sonnets to date, insofar as we can date them, with its enactment of the speaker's emotional state: by the third quatrain, as he *grieve[s] at grievances*, self-denigration escalates into self-mockery through the poem's third and fourth uses of *woe*, its second and third moans, its keeping of the ledger (*expense . . . sad account . . . new pay . . . not paid*). Relief—reversal—comes in the entrance of another character (*dear friend*), as welcome an action as Juliet's. Increasingly as the style matures, and throughout the middle sonnets that set the paradigm, one can hear beautifully shaped twelve-line soliloquies, the hero perhaps strapping on his sword, shoring up his resolve. In #116, for instance, the couplet seems simply an afterthought, two lines tossed over his shoulder as he exits:

> Let me not to the marriage of true minds
> Admit impediments. Love is not love
> Which alters when it alteration finds,
> Or bends with the remover to remove:
> O, no! it is an ever-fixèd mark
> That looks on tempests and is never shaken;
> It is the star to every wandering bark,
> Whose worth's unknown, although his height be taken.
> Love's not Time's fool, though rosy lips and cheeks
> Within his bending sickle's compass come;
> Love alters not with his brief hours and weeks,
> But bears it out even to the edge of doom.
>   If this be error and upon me proved,
>   I never writ, nor no man ever loved.

Gilbert Murray trusts that no one will "imagine that . . . insistence on the element of tradition in Shakespeare . . . affects
in the smallest degree the greatness of [the] poet's genius. It is
one of the very feeblest of critical errors to suppose that there
is a thing called 'originality,' which consists in having no models." We mean by the word, I suppose, the boldness required to
draw potions from allegedly incompatible vats and make of them
some surprising new composite. But then that composite becomes a vat as well. It will be a long time (not until Milton, by
and large) before such boldness again addresses the English sonnet. Even absent a dependable dating of the poems, my own narrative detects the now familiar formula everywhere, high and low.
The tinkering in the various labs is with form, not structure[10]—
Shakespeare's own controversial #145 is in tetrameter ("Those
lips that love's own hand did make"). It is hard not to think that
the master chemist parodied his own discovery, and its popularity, in #130:

> My mistress' eyes are nothing like the sun;
> Coral is far more red than her lips' red;
> If snow be white, why then her breasts are dun;
> If hairs be wires, black wires grow on her head.
> I have seen roses damask'd, red and white,
> But no such roses see I in her cheeks;
> And in some perfumes is there more delight
> Than in the breath that from my mistress reeks.
> I love to hear her speak, yet well I know
> That music hath a far more pleasing sound;
> I grant I never saw a goddess go;
> My mistress, when she walks, treads on the ground:
> And yet, by heaven, I think my love as rare
> As any she belied with false compare.

The tone here could have been plucked straight out of *Much Ado
about Nothing* or *As You Like It*.

But even self-parody has its uses. One of Shakespeare's greatest sonnets, #129, is thought these days to be one of the last four

he wrote—a plausible claim: in it, he pushes past the quatrain independence of his own achievement, employing all his now characteristic rhetorical, syntactic, sonic, and metrical patterns toward construction of a seamless twelve-line unit, its interior so formally rich that attention is forced away from the end rhyme and its subdivisions:

> Th'expense of spirit in a waste of shame
> Is lust in action; and till action, lust
> Is perjured, murderous, bloody, full of blame,
> Savage, extreme, rude, cruel, not to trust;
> Enjoyed no sooner but despisèd straight:
> Past reason hunted; and no sooner had,
> Past reason hated, as a swallowed bait,
> On purpose laid to make the taker mad:
> Mad in pursuit, and in possession so;
> Had, having, and in quest to have, extreme;
> A bliss in proof, and proved, a very woe;
> Before, a joy proposed; behind, a dream.
> All this the world well knows; yet none knows well
> To shun the heaven that leads men to this hell.

This may seem a very compendium of Aristotle's *Art of Rhetoric*, and a brilliant one at that. But as Richard Lewontin has noted, although Aristotle "deftly swallowed Plato by including within rhetoric both a recitation of the evidence and the logical structure of argument based on the facts," "artful language creates its own logic" and is "[m]any times more dangerous."[11] Despite the high ratio of rhetoric to image in the texture (the "evidence"), the organizational principle at work in #129 is not argumentation but association. What it charts, perhaps anticipating *Hamlet*, is obsession, scored as an aria (*perjured, murderous, bloody, full of blame / Savage, extreme, rude, cruel, not to trust*). And paradox has not been reserved for contradiction in the final two lines; throughout, the poem's two central moments— *before* and *behind*—are welded together in a single intolerable condition, as the *bliss* of *having* gets barely a prepositional nod (*in action, in possession, in proof*). With line 12 restoring us to the tonic chord, the couplet withers away into a kind of weary punctuation.

The step from a few strategically placed enjambments to a preponderance of them, from associative structure to narrative sequence, from a two-line self-evident closure to a single line, is a small one:

> The little Love-god lying once asleep
> Laid by his side his heart-inflaming brand,
> Whilst many nymphs that vow'd chaste life to keep
> Came tripping by; but in her maiden hand
> The fairest votary took up that fire
> Which many legions of true hearts had warm'd;
> And so the general of hot desire
> Was sleeping by a virgin hand disarm'd.
> This brand she quenched in a cool well by,
> Which from Love's fire took heat perpetual,
> Growing a bath and healthful remedy
> For men diseased; but I, my mistress' thrall,
> Came there for cure, and this by that I prove,
> Love's fire heats water, water cools not love.
>
> (Shakespeare, Sonnet 154; generally considered
> his last known sonnet, though regarded by some
> as a very early exercise)

And when that step moves the poet more completely into idiom and character, as is the case at what seems the cycle's end, the next step is smaller still: to the utter replacement of *logos* with *pathos*, of end rhyme with an interior music, irony now enacting paradox throughout. And what happens to the couplet, that most "Shakespearean" legacy? The dramatist replaces it with efficient action: watch for Edmund's swift conclusion to and reversal of King Lear's final monologue in act 5, scene 3, which is set in "the British camp near Dover. Enter, in conquest, with drum and colours, Edmund; Lear and Cordelia, prisoners; Captain, Soldiers, etc."

    EDM.   Some officers take them away: good guard,
             Until their greater pleasures first be known
             That are to censure them.
    COR.   We are not the first
             Who, with best meaning, have incurr'd the worst.
             For thee, oppressed king, am I cast down;
             Myself could else out-frown false fortune's frown.
             Shall we not see these daughters and these sisters?
    LEAR. No, no, no, no! Come, let's away to prison:
             We two alone will sing like birds i' the cage:
             When thou dost ask me blessing, I'll kneel down,
             And ask of thee forgiveness; so we'll live,
             And pray, and sing, and tell old tales, and laugh
             At gilded butterflies, and hear poor rogues
             Talk of court news; and we'll talk with them too,
             Who loses and who wins; who's in, who's out;
             And take upon's the mystery of things,
             As if we were God's spies; and we'll wear out,
             In a wall'd prison, packs and sects of great ones,
             That ebb and flow by the moon.
    EDM.   Take them away.

III

In the eighteenth century, naturalists commonly used a classification of "quadrupeds" which excluded lizards and salamanders but included bats and walruses, liberties no longer needed once the class was renamed "mammal."[12] My proposal for a structural definition of lyric means to counter, with Shakespeare's Darwinian varieties, a purely formal definition—the lyric as quadruped. In place of Ransom's dialectic and Brooks's hierarchy I have argued that a poem's structure, form, and texture are made of the same words and vowels, repetitions, and even meters, and that the important differences lie in the distinct functions to which such materials are put. Susanne Langer catalogues them as the strategies by which poetry's "import" joins matter and manner, the assertion of the words and "the way the assertion is made,"

> the sound, the tempo, the aura of association of words, the long or short sequences of ideas, the wealth or poverty of transient image that contains them[;] the sudden arrest of fantasy by pure fact, or of familiar fact by sudden fantasy, the suspense of literal meaning by a sustained ambiguity resolved in a long awaited key-word[;] and the unifying, all-embracing artifice of rhythm. (*Philosophy in a New Key*)

My altered punctuation underscores the strategies: comparative, evaluative descriptors—*long/short, wealth/poverty*—suggest the textural impact of sound, tempo, words, ideas, image; the references to timing and pacing—*sudden, suspense, sustained, resolved, long awaited, key-word*—a structural function; and *unifying, all-embracing artifice*, form's proportion, its right relation of all the parts.

Langer's point, of course, is their interrelation, their presentational (rather than discursive) nature, the result, in the completed work, of something like Ransom's foot-on-the-gas, foot-on-the-clutch interchange of meaning and sound. A rudimentary example may be seen in some of Kenneth Koch's exercises, which invite schoolchildren to elaborate a "poem idea" or fixed formal pattern.[13] Another sequence may occur as well: some compelling textural fragment may trigger composition ("stirrings," Seamus Heaney calls it), the determinate element or *donné* only an aspect of tone, or an indelible image, which then opens suddenly visible patterns or effective organization. A more elaborate example can be found, perhaps, in the extent to which the Shakespearean *volta*, delayed from Petrarch's octave to a final couplet, coincided in his sonnet sequence with the emergence of specific textural characteristics we call Shakespearean. The sequence, in composition, of the poet's attention to texture, structure, and form must remain variable, opportunistic, temperamental, "with strokes too subtle and rapid to record . . . [as] the poet makes adaptations both of sound to meaning . . . and of meaning to sound" (Ransom, "Wanted"). Nevertheless, asking where, in a completed poem, texture has been used in the service of structure, where for formal arrangement, can prove useful when tracking the lyric into the free-verse thicket.

Here's the present difficulty: the record of lyric evolution, from words performed to the music of the lyre to written document to expanding adaptations (ballad, sonnet, public and private odes), long ago became a taxonomy of verse forms—formal conventions and exoskeletal structures—which, like those silhouettes of birds in the field guide, no longer seems very helpful out in the field, with new species on the wing or in the nest. Eschewing patterns that Murray called "emphatic to the ear," poets must pay even more attention to enjambment and end stop if lines are to maintain a necessary relation to syntax and speech stress—although many poets don't. Even prose poems need rhythmic patterns and sonic construction, only depending more heavily on syntax than does metrical verse; at the same time, the self-styled L=A=N=G=U=A=G=E poets undermine and overturn syntax. If all this is harder on the watchers than the birds, birds nevertheless learn their songs by hearing them. Once released from the old conventions, according to Jonathan Holden, contemporary poets simply developed a new set: poem addressing a painting or photograph, poem in the form of a letter, and so on. Meanwhile, syllabic meter, rhyme, and highly artificial verse forms such as the sestina enjoy resurgence, alongside sniping at free-verse handball courts, which lack Frost's metrical tennis net.

I'll make a long aside, here, to admit unseemly optimism regarding the American poetry wars. Now that democratization is so thoroughly accomplished, poets are freed from the shadow of a single overwhelming figure, and freed as well from a dominant aesthetic, from the hegemony of theorists (for whom actual poets are mainly irrelevant), from the old hierarchy of publishers (while most of the large ones have abandoned poetry altogether, small presses print more volumes of poetry than ever before), and from the tyranny of reviewers (most newspapers and journals no longer review poetry at all, unless it's in translation). The general population prefers television to literature, and any idealism about increasing poetry's esteem in the culture faded with the last earnest, futile antiwar readings that preceded Kent State and the bombing of Cambodia. With so little remuneration from poetry (and it was ever thus), and more American poets than ever before (for which Poets-in-the-Schools and MFA programs continue to be chastised), one might say poets now have nothing to lose and everything at stake—a wonderfully inchoate leisure in which to figure out what, with free verse, we were freed FOR.

It has also produced a snappish sibling rivalry, as happens with too much lying-about-the-house, and poets intent on traditional verse are roundly accused, by free-verse brethren, of retrograde, right-wing politics. But aren't they more like Wyatt and Surrey, trying to adapt, for our own time and language, something received, glorious, if not quite compatible? Theirs may indeed be a nostalgic solution: after all, while others waste time in the murk of poetry versus prose, "[t]he difference between *verse* and prose is self-evident" (Auden; my italics). But the more pernicious nostalgia lies not in overt regularity, since all art requires some measure of pattern and variation, and not in Dennis's "openness to tradition," the ground from which even the avant garde (surely they want it there for everyone else) must spring, but in the accompanying disregard for "the organization of a good poem, so full of strain and tension, . . . obtained not merely by intensifying the forces working toward a simple unity, but by intensifying the opposing forces as well" (Jarrell). When meter is honored over rhythm, line over syntax, form over structure, even the most prodigious manipulation of traditional patterns may be rendered purely decorative.

I should make clear that "decorative" is a judgment made about a lack of function in the formal patterning, not about the patterns themselves, and that it does not imply a stylistic bias. I do not equate fixed meters and rhyme, on the one hand, with high style and sonority—an equation implicit in many attacks, such as Joseph Epstein's in *Commonweal*, on low-style free-verse poems. This reading of tradition IS reactionary, in precisely the way Auden described:

> The English-speaking peoples have always felt that the differ-
> ence between poetic speech and the conversational speech
> of everyday should be kept small, and, whenever English
> poets have felt that the gap between poetic and ordinary
> speech was growing too wide, there has been a stylistic revo-
> lution to bring them closer again. In English verse, even in
> Shakespeare's grandest rhetorical passages, the ear is always
> aware of its relation to everyday speech. . . . [I]f [one] tries to
> make the verse sound like a different language, he will make
> himself ridiculous. (*The Dyer's Hand*)

Whatever their hapless convergence with critics' taste, the Neo-formalists' project seems trying not at all to counter that "stylis-tic revolution" but to find, in formal means, some pitons for scal-ing the flat, slick walls of its idiom and discourse. My own resistance to their program (which is no doubt more heteroge-neous than advertised) is twofold: that "formal means" is nar-rowly defined, and that so few of their members have Richard Wilbur's ear. Poems of contemporary voice merely willed into quantifiable verse, with unvaried, arhythmic meter or predictable rhymes, seem as static, as inert, as discarded mollusk shells—al-though the same may be said of many free-verse slugs as well.

In successful poems, of course, form has always encompassed far more than rhyme or meter, and open or organic form has never meant NO form. Finally, isn't the function of the formal ap-paratus, traditional or not, more to the point than the choice of apparatus? Whether we are neo-Surreys, nascent Shakespeares, or even, as charged, a cluster of far lesser lights, genre awareness couldn't fail to be instructive in this regard. But the notions about lyric have undergone such radical contractions and expansions that a new generation of poets has come along with either a pejorative sense of what a lyric is or no sense at all.

At the 1979 Breadloaf Writers Conference, Stanley Plumly gave a lecture recommending "narrative values" for poetry. From here one can see that his talk was riding a pendulum swing, both a reaction against Confessionalism and a furthering of its premises. In the dim readings of the label rather than the actual contents, lyric had come to be associated firmly with feeling but no longer also with thought, largely with song but no longer also with speech. The gnarled inwardness of Berryman, Plath, and Lowell would be replaced as a model by the genial clarity of their contemporary, Elizabeth Bishop, while the autobiographical ground they had broken would be further harrowed by neonarrative practitioners. Lyric seemed, in a word, solipsistic. "Narrative values" made a poem more ambitious, more flexible, more commodious, distinguishing the greater achievement of "Among Schoolchildren" from "Sailing to Byzantium," in Plumly's view. And, we might note, they informed the "Robinsonian technique of telling a story in a short lyric" praised by Mark Jarman in the December 1997 *AWP Chronicle*.

Since Pound, poets have increasingly sought the advantages of prose in their poems, including highly idiomatic diction and extended syntax as well as a loosened or displaced metric. And contemporary poems have increasingly displayed the very texture Plumly recommended: bits of discursive meditation, overt dramatic situation, narrative summary, small sequences of action verbs, and convincingly circumstantial detail.[14] But Shakespeare's sonnets demonstrate that such textural borrowings were frequent in even our earliest lyrics. Nor, likewise, has poetic narrative lacked the musical devices common to the lyric poem. As with the use of conventional forms, relying on texture seems as limited a method of genre classification as grouping plants by the color of their blossoms.[15]

A case in point is Denise Levertov's unrhymed, nonmetrical, endoskeletal poem:

Sunday Afternoon

After the First Communion,
and the banquet of mangoes and
bridal cake, the young daughters
of the coffee merchant lay down
for a long siesta, and their white dresses
lay beside them in quietness
and the white veils floated
in their dreams as the flies buzzed.
But as the afternoon
burned to a close they rose
and ran about the neighborhood
among the halfbuilt villas
alive, alive, kicking a basketball, wearing
other new dresses of bloodred velvet.

A first look at "Sunday Afternoon" perhaps would place it at some nether textural pole from the Renaissance sonnets, and perhaps under some other genre flag. The poem seems to be told to us, not overheard. We have a removed, informed speaker who stays thoroughly behind the third-person-plural pronoun; the diction is relaxed and idiomatic, spiced here and there with the exotica of a foreign country—*mangoes, siesta, villas*. The syntax is fluid, natural, draped casually across the lineation. What rhyme exists is buried—*white/quiet, cake/lay/veils, banquet/basket-/ velvet, dresses/quietness*—with the exception of *close/rose* in line 10. As is true of most effective prose narrative, it is arranged in scenes—in this case, two in chronological sequence: early and late afternoon.

By now, contemporary theory having divested poems of intentionality and even of authorship (revealing instead the culture speaking from behind the curtain), it's common enough to speak of poems morphing freely from lyric into narrative or drama and back again, these terms usually meant to describe only texture, "lyric" an adjective interchangeable with "lyrical" to mean "song-like," "poetic." But a poem's structure is where intentionality still stubbornly resides. The relationship of Levertov's two scenes is one we've seen before. What they do not reveal is any differentiation among the characters—are there two daughters? five? a dozen? Is one dreamy and tender, another one feisty and difficult? Where does the story or drama take place? Should we know something about the politics there, the class status of "the coffee merchant"? And what about the domestic politics? Did the father bring the basketball home to his girls? In the course of the poem's "chronology," has there been significant change in these plural characters; or, next week, will the same transformation be undergone? Which is to say, does the time sequence have narrative consequence?

Despite the "narrative values" in its texture, the poem's concerns are elsewhere: with the aspects of experience held in common by young women coming into physical and sensual maturation, including both the "sleep" of virginal innocence and an awakening to physical passion. The afternoon of the title represents any given moment of their adolescence, but any day would do: the Sunday of First Communion is metaphorical, synecdochical, used to structure the argument and present the paradox. Sequence matters only in its analogue: in maturation, girls move from sexual innocence to sexual pleasure, from a marriage to Christ to an earthly marriage. The poem itself marries two strophes, each one roughly half of the predicament.

This is, of course, the structure of the Petrarchan sonnet without its formal conventions. Although there is no regular meter to unify the fourteen lines, no rhyme scheme to divide them into octave and sestet, syntax signals that same arrangement of material. The opening eight lines establish the first proposition in one long sentence; its period, the poem's second end stop, marks octave from sestet. These lines take place, dramatically, in one location (indoors), and at the same thematic moment (after the First Communion). Following the conjunction *But*, which announces the *volta*, the last six lines, again a single sentence, occur at a later moment (*But as the afternoon burned to a close*) and outdoors, in the physical world. Reflecting a radical change as quick—and as impermanent, at that age—as a change of clothes, and as alien as new costume, images of innocence are grouped in the octave (*bridal cake, white dresses, quietness, white veils floating in their dreams*), those of passion in the sestet (*burned, alive, kicking, bloodred velvet*).

There are also supporting shifts of diction and tone. All that is Catholic, Spanish, and traditional appears in the octave: *Communion, banquet, mangoes, bridal cake, coffee merchant, siesta, white dresses, white veils*, the dreamed (and ideal) life. In the sestet, except for the *villas* (which are, like the girls, *halfbuilt* and thus as new as the velvet dresses), the diction turns contemporary (*basketball*) and geographically neutral (*neighborhood*). As the patronymic noun (*daughters*) is replaced by generalized pronoun (*they*) and the girls are freed from tradition into sensuality, the pace shifts. There are very few verbs in the first eight lines, and those are inactive (*lay down, lay, floated*); the change begins with those flies that buzz at the end of the octave and anticipate the sestet where *afternoon burned, they rose, ran, kicking, wearing*. The dream is ended; the daughters "come alive" in the "real" life (flies being more dependable presences than dreams) of the sestet.

In other words, the formal arrangements of syntax, diction, and image make patterns in the texture which are organized to create the poem's Janus-face looking back and then forward, enacting the paradox of female adolescence—in Brooklyn, in Colorado, in India. Setting and event function as metaphors, vivid and economical, containing as they do identifiable and suggestive elements of tradition and ritual. Nothing happens in the poem as a result of who the characters are, where they live, what they do; there are none of the important variables of narrative. Is this poem a sonnet? One could argue that it is—that Levertov welds Petrarchan structure to formal experiment for the sake of idiom, much as the first English sonneteers did—but that would be arguing about form and about the loyalty to convention required for the label. What seems inarguable is that it is a lyric. Beneath its relaxed surface the structure reveals the poem's reach for the universal through lyric's compression and juxtaposition rather than narrative's tracking of character and circumstance.

John Berryman's Dreamsong #29, discussed earlier in regard to tone, may seem either more clearly a lyric or less, depending on where one looks for genre definition.

> There sat down, once, a thing on Henry's heart
> so heavy, if he had a hundred years
> & more, & weeping, sleepless, in all them time
> Henry could not make good.
> Starts again always in Henry's ears
> the little cough somewhere, an odour, a chime.
>
> And there is another thing he has in mind
> like a grave Sienese face a thousand years
> would fail to blur the still profiled reproach of. Ghastly,
> with open eyes, he attends, blind.
> All the bells say: too late. This is not for tears;
> thinking.
>
> But never did Henry, as he thought he did,
> end anyone and hacks her body up
> and hide the pieces, where they may be found.
> He knows: he went over everyone, & nobody's missing.
> Often he reckons, in the dawn, them up.
> Nobody is ever missing.

Our first response surely must be to the tone: that is, the composite formed by the texture, the sound of the feeling, "the way the assertion [of the words] is made" (as Langer puts it). In Dreamsong #29 we hear something both more bitter and more puzzled than the self-denigrating accounting of Shakespeare's #30 ("When to the sessions . . .") or the self-laceration of his #129 ("Th'expense of spirit . . .")—and those tonal differences are lodged, in poems of similar dilemma, in the differences in diction, syntax, and music.

In poems as in conversation, word choices (erudite or slangy, precise or dreamy, neutral or loaded) and word order (acquired by children before a full lexicon) tell us something about the speaker and provide affect for what is said. Berryman's Dreamsong #29 offers an immensely varied diction, combining latinate words (*profiled reproach*) with burlesque blackface (*in all them time*), and these wild juxtapositions provide not only energy and momentum but a complex tonal field. The musical control is, meanwhile, expert. For instance, as Berryman brings the poem to a close, his diction becomes increasingly plain-spoken but within strained syntax:

> He knows: he went over everyone, & nobody's missing.
> Often he reckons, in the dawn, them up.
> Nobody is ever missing.

Not a fancy word in the bunch. What stands out is *reckons*, idiomatic for supposition and also figuring, doing elementary math—an endearing word. But whereas the first sentence is direct and compound, a natural speaking order, the second, instead of putting the parenthetical adverbial phrase in some unobtrusive place—Often in the dawn he reckons them up; or, Often he reckons them up in the dawn—jams it between the verb and its direct object, stalling the line at the one odd touch of diction (*reckons*) with its medial hard *K*. The poem is slowed in other ways, too: instead of lineation AGAINST those elaborate sentences insinuating down the page, we suddenly have one full sentence per line; and end rhyme, earlier enjambed or forgone, is replaced by direct end-stopped repetition. The final exacting replacement of the idiomatically elided letter—*nobody's missing. . . . / Nobody is ever missing*—locks in a texture of intense despair, a tone of numb, enforced recognition.

Just as the presence of a plausible third-person character would make a weak case for this as narrative, however, Berryman's overt musical devices don't necessarily distract the poem FROM narrative the way, for instance, anaphora, parallel syntax, and end stops do in Whitman, providing pattern's leash for texture's pack of dogs; in Berryman such effects are too independent, too opportunistic. As the diction swings widely, the syntax shifts from simple and declarative to inverted to truncated and back again as the poet chooses, freely mixing imagery and statement. A more overt pattern of formal elements, such as rhyme and meter, could have served stability, as in Shakespeare's Sonnet 129, but rhyme here is often hidden or elided, and line lengths vary. And to note these characteristics, these textural fingerprints, in other Dreamsongs merely notes the poet's style: texture no more surely indicates genre allegiance than it did in Levertov.

Ignore for a moment the length of the poem, the fixed stanzaic divisions, the irregular line units. Ignore also the genre-borrowing mode of the Berryman sentences, the way they alternate expository, dramatic, and narrative information. And ignore those idiosyncrasies of diction. The stuff the poem brings into language—the "truth" it wishes to convince Auden's skeptical reader of—is endless self-recrimination. As in "Sunday Afternoon" and the Renaissance sonnets, the poem's materials are organized into two contradictory premises: Henry's guilt suggests a crime, but (*volta*) there is no hard evidence that he has committed one. Like Sidney's Sonnet 31 ("With how sad steps, Oh Moon . . .") the poem begins with effect, with condition, and moves toward discovery of cause—only here, absence of cause. With so much inverted or convoluted syntax, we clutch at the declarative statements and want to make of them a narrative sequence:

> There sat down once . . .
> Henry could not make good . . .
> Starts again . . .

> But never did Henry . . .
> he went over everyone . . .
> Often he reckons them up . . .

But although the impact of this information on the reader depends on this particular order of its release—on the redundancy and the sly time references (*once, never, often, ever*)—nothing else does: the statements all refer to the same or a recurring moment in time. Even as he hears the little cough, the chime, as he attends, as he reckons them up, Henry *knows* he has not murdered anyone. Reversing the two premises changes only the dramatic force of the reader's epiphany—which is to say, the "story line" does not function structurally. Nor should it. This is a lyric, delivering one unalterable dilemma and its pain: that guilt does not require commission.

To what extent does the form reinforce the structure, as in "exoskeletal" Renaissance pieces? Berryman uses a stanzaic division of three parts; the first two stanzas set out the problem, the third stanza snatches away resolution. The Petrarchan sonnet divides neatly into octave and sestet, and the octave is halved as quatrains, in Sidney's poem the second quatrain working to elaborate and further refine the premise of the first (the moon as brother in love's misery). Berryman likewise follows assertion with elaboration, using end-stopped stanzas of six lines rather than four. By convention, the two quatrains are bound by rhyme; Berryman also links the first and second stanzas of his poem by mirroring the alternating (Shakespearean) rhyme:

heart	—
years	*a*
time	*b*
good	—
ears	*a*
chime	*b*
mind	*b*
years	*a*

ghastly	—
blind	*b*
tears	*a*
thinking	—

There is even the Petrarchan interlocking couplet between units (*chime/mind*). In the third stanza, after the Petrarchan *volta* (*But never did Henry . . .*), Berryman shifts, as is usual, to a new set of sounds and an altered pattern, this one full of stubborn reiteration:

did	*d*
up	*e*
found	*d'*
missing	*f*
up	*e*
missing	*f*

Pulling against the tidy stanzas, of course, are the tremendous —one might say Dionysian—textural variety and the structure: not the consequential order of narrative event but the "qualitative progression" which moves the poem, releasing its emotional information, as relentlessly as Shakespeare's Sonnet 73 ("That time of year . . ."). We open with *a thing* on Henry's heart—a generalized threat rendered more precise by the nouns ending the stanza: *cough, odour, chime*. The cough is further humanized in stanza 2 with a face and a profile, but we lapse back with the chime, now enlarged, louder—*All the bells say*—and a pronoun (*This*) even more vague than the repeated noun (*thing*). The *volta* turns us suddenly and drastically—to *her* body, *anyone, everyone, nobody, nobody*, his putative victim now human and female.

A similar progression of intensity rules out atonement. *If he had a hundred years, & more*, says stanza 1, Henry *could not make good*; in stanza 2 *a thousand years* is no longer enough; in the sestet, *never, ever* can he be absolved. Henry's responses are constructed too. First this thing is on his heart and in his ears and nose—something he senses; in stanza 2 he is blind, but it persists *in mind* (*This is . . . for . . . thinking*); the final sestet leaps to absolute knowledge. Likewise, whereas Henry is paralyzed and conditional in the first stanza, passive in the second (his only verbs are *has* and *attends*), there is a frenzy of activity in the last stanza, both imagined (*end anyone and hacks her body up / and hide the pieces*) and actual (*He knows: he went over everyone, he reckons them up*).

The experience of the poem for the reader is movement, toward resolution if not revelation. The experience in the poem for Henry is fixed, unrelieved, a constant condition—each stanza with its reminder (*sleepless, open eyes, in the dawn*)—which having happened *once* happens *again, always, too late, forever.* This is the exact understanding of guilt: if atonement seems possible, we aren't feeling guilty. And this is the tight focus which empowers the compressed lyric, which looks steadily at a leaf and sees the tree; it depends on microcosm and it works by analogue. The use of a character—Henry—provides Berryman the terms of the vehicle, just as First Communion functioned in Levertov's poem, and this choice, whatever its narrative suggestions or its dramatic possibilities, serves a deeply lyric purpose.

Such an allegiance has nothing to do with convention. Substitute, for instance, the conventional lyric pronoun in that last stanza:

But never did I, as I thought I did,
end anyone and hack her body up
and hide the pieces . . .

The change DECREASES lyric intensity, giving us neurosis rather than obsession and deflecting our own capability for violent murder by consigning it to the crazies. Choice of pronoun is never generic, whatever the genre.

Stephen Dobyns is a poet well aware of his options, having also written serious novels, mystery novels, stories, essays, and journalism. "Fragments" is a poem quite shrewd in its use of pronouns. It appears in his third book, *Heat Death* (1980), alongside such memorable early narratives as "The Delicate, Plummeting Bodies," "Fear," and "Pablo Neruda," and its texture is full of narrative gestures.

> Now there is a slit in the blue fabric of air.
> His house spins faster. He holds down books,
> chairs; his life and its objects fly upward:
> vanishing black specks in the indifferent sky.
>
> The sky is a torn piece of blue paper.
> He tries to repair it, but the memory
> of death is like paste on his fingers
> and certain days stick like dead flies.
>
> Say the sky goes back to being the sky
> and the sun continues as always. Now, knowing
> what you know, how can you not see thin
> cracks in the fragile blue vaults of air?
>
> My friend, what can I give you or darkness
> lift from you but fragments of language,
> fragments of blue sky. You had three
> beautiful daughters and one has died.

The formal arrangement provides four stanzas of equal length, with generally equivalent line lengths. Alert to the Petrarchan bivalve, we may note the apparent division exactly midway in the poem, at line 9. Each of the first two quatrains announces extremity, then falls back to a man's response to it, all rendered dispassionately in uncluttered, simple declarative sentences and unpretentious, accessible diction. The third quatrain changes the texture with a hypothesized remedy and imperative syntax:

> Say the sky goes back to being the sky . . .

A listener is implied here, a "you" made explicit in the interrogative that follows. Further, the colloquialism (*Say the sky* . . .) and the intensity—either impatience or sadness—in the question

(*how can you not see* . . .) suggest a connection between the protagonist and the speaker. The eight-eight division seems also reinforced by a rudimentary plot: the man's useless activity in the
first two quatrains (holding down his books and chairs, trying to
repair the sky) diminishes in the last two (*knowing what you
know, you had* are statements of fact ABOUT him, framing two
anguished questions put TO him), even as the wizard/speaker
emerges from behind the screen.

But something subterranean is working in tension with the
eight-eight formal division, something not unlike Shakespeare's
second *volta* in the early sonnets. Each of Dobyns's first three
stanzas refers to the universe—sky and air—and the damage
done to it, increasingly severe: *slit, torn, cracked*. Each stanza reminds us of precariousness—*fabric, paper, fragile vaults*. In a
progression of metaphors the man's responses slide steadily into
futility, from attempts at prevention which fail (he holds down
objects, but still they fly upward), to attempts at repair which fail,
to acknowledgment of permanent helplessness (*cracks in the
fragile blue vaults of air*).

The significant turn in the poem comes with the fourth stanza:
My friend, the speaker says, marking the first crucial change in
the kind of information being released—the emotional invest-
ment of the speaker—and a shift in tone. Another's tragedy feels
contagious, and the damage described in the first three stanzas
may apply also to how tragic news *slits, tears*, then *cracks* the
speaker's own sense of a stable universe. In the first stanza's
Olympian point of view, the friend is an almost comic figure,
Dorothy spinning toward Oz and grabbing onto the furniture.
Stanza 2 carries, in the poem's two similes (paste, dead flies), a
scent of the superiority one feels toward the pathetic. And the
syntax in stanza 3 is pushy—is there an edge of anger because his
friend has shoved death under his nose? With the more compassionate address and the more formal syntax that follows it, danger and pain are returned to the friend as the speaker admits his
own helplessness.

Like a Shakespearean couplet, Dobyns's final stanza summarizes and reveals. The first three lines—

My friend, what can I give you or darkness
lift from you but fragments of language,
fragments of blue sky.

—reprise and condense the movement, no longer vicarious, of the initial two quatrains, from willful action into defeat, while offering the poem's first "I": the poet with his futile bag of tricks, now revealed explicitly in the relationship only implied earlier. The *indifferent sky*, around which each stanza has been organized, is no longer embroidered by figure (the recurring *blue* helps us chart them—*fabric, paper, vaults*) but is left inchoate (*fragments* recalled from the title twice in parallel phrases) and as a child might paint it: *blue sky*. And what seemed hyperbole is unmasked as analogue, as Prospero packs up his kit and moves quickly, bluntly, to confirm despair:

You had three
beautiful daughters and one has died.

This last piece of information is what the speaker and his friend have known all along: the revelation comes only to the reader. The story is a tool, a device: chronology has no meaning here. As in the Levertov and Berryman poems, events do not occur on a linear continuum. In Dobyns's poem there is only "after": since the daughter cannot be replaced, the universe is permanently changed; the entire poem occurs at that one moment, which is to say all succeeding moments (suggested by the declarative syntax and active verbs) thereafter. Is Dobyns's protagonist sentimental or intelligent, likable or obnoxious? Does he drink beer or kick the dog? And which of the daughters died—youngest, oldest, middle? How old was she? How did she die? The lyric need not tell us. Event and action here are figurative; inference and tonal resonance replace narrative information. Through compression and song, pattern and variation, Dobyns structures an argument; the poem does not lack particulars, but they are more specific to grief than to this illustrative one-who-grieves, and the poem thereby asserts that *x* will always be true: the loss of a child will always destroy one's universe. Even as the "single effect" of the formal patterns points us TO the example, structure points us out FROM the example to the macrocosm the example implies, and the opposing centripetal and centrifugal forces keep the poem aloft in its orbit.

According to Randall Jarrell, a successful poem "starts from one position and ends at a very different one, often a contradictory or opposite one; yet there has been no break in the unity of the poem. This unity is generated by the tension set up between strongly differing forces, by the struggle of opposites[,] . . . a unity that is arrived at through heterogeneity." Although he tries "to avoid the mistake of saying that poetry, or good poetry, or the best poetry, is always dialectical," he is quite clear that a worse mistake is to "think of poetic structure as the mere unifying of the poem" and thereby give form "an altogether disproportionate amount of attention." Furthermore, "organization, in its widest sense, is more difficult and—almost—more important than anything else in the poem, because it more nearly than anything else corresponds to the whole that *is* the poem" ("Levels and Opposites").

Structures that accommodate paradox, like those in the Berryman, Levertov, and Dobyns poems, not only support Jarrell's brief but also illustrate how perception can be singular and multiple simultaneously. This last is characteristic of (but not limited to) feeling and goes to the heart of (but does not limit) the lyric project: a moment lifted out of time but not static; movement that is centripetal and centrifugal rather than linear; an examination of self which discovers universal predicament; insight embodied in individuated particulars and at the same time overriding them. In successful lyric poems these priorities subordinate the reader's appetite for story, which arises, as in life, from permutations of character and circumstance. And structures most compatible with these priorities need not restrict a writer's "freedom," since "the impulse to modify the tradition is built into the tradition itself" (Dennis).

Such is the "grandeur" Darwin recognized, that "whilst this planet has gone cycling on according to the fixed law of gravity, from so simple a beginning endless forms most beautiful and wonderful have been, and are being, evolved" (*The Origin of Species*).

Notes

1. Both of them ever courtly, Brooks deflects his disagreement with Ransom onto Winters's more rigid application of similar precepts, just as Ransom feels free in "deprecating Warren's argument" for its insistence on a "systematic interrelationship of all of [poetry's] components" ("Positive"), while omitting Brooks's name from his "Address to Kenneth Burke":

> I read respected authors, and I have friends, who seem to me to misplace, and bring up on the wrong occasions, their admiration for harmony, and for such adjunct excellences as reconciliation, resolution, synthesis, unification, and plain unity. . . . In a scientific process there is harmony in the way the extended parts fit themselves spatially and temporally together, and the way each does its little bit of work for the whole and does nothing on its own account; which is unity, logico-mathematical harmony. But no harmony exists logico-mathematically among the heterogeneous properties of a natural object. You can compose separate apples into a nice total weight or volume or quota or money value or geometrical row or Christmas design of apples, but how can you compose a red and a sweet and a round and a heavy into one apple? To assemble the original properties is the work of nature, and the assemblage, if we think about it, always strikes us as arbitrary and contingent, a pure gift or datum, which reason cannot understand though sense witnesses it indubitably.

He will address Brooks directly but respectfully in 1952 ("Why Critics Don't Go Mad").

2. Randall Jarrell's "Levels and Opposites: Structure in Poetry"—uncollected and unpublished, only recently discovered and printed in the *Georgia Review* (Winter 1996)—followed by one year Ransom's own lecture, "Criticism as Pure Speculation," in the Princeton series. Surprisingly for Jarrell, it treats no texts. This may mean that it was an early take he planned to revisit or may suggest some hesitancy about joining the argument between two important mentors.

3. There is a clear discussion of this—and of Chomsky's universal grammar, Broca's area in the brain, Piagetian acquisition, and much else—in Steven Pinker's *The Language Instinct* (1995). One Pinker example of unconscious branching is the following aphorism: "Time flies like an arrow; fruit flies like a banana." Others, and the resulting puns and ambiguity, are these newspaper headlines:

Stud Tires Out
Deer Kill 130,000
Hershey Bars Protest
Chou Remains Cremated

"Mental dictionary lookup," Pinker notes, "is quick and thorough but not very bright; it retrieves nonsensical entries that must be weeded out later."

4. The brain's centers for music appear even less "lateralized" than those for language, though not always distinct from them. A relevant lay translation of this research is available in Robert Jourdain's *Music, the Brain, and Ecstasy: How Music Captures Our Imagination* (1997), chap. 9.

5. An equally plausible explanation, however, is the similarity of Wyatt's variation to rhyme royal (*ababbcc*), already used elegantly in English verse by Chaucer and Spenser, among others.

6. One example of this may be seen in the exceptional Shakespeare Sonnet 94, a poem of fifteen lines. The dramatic situation (a flower is being addressed), necessary to understanding the metaphor, is simply announced in a prefatory line that serves as a kind of title ("The forward violet thus did I chide") and the initial quatrain extended to incorporate it (*ababa*).

7. Wyatt's "The long love that in my thought doth harbor"; Surrey's "Love, that doth reign and live within my thought."

8. There is, for instance, Sonnet 126 ("O thou, my lovely boy, who

in thy power")—twelve lines, six couplets—excluded from the 1640 volume.

9. Something should be said about the disputed dates of the sonnets. I have my own quibbles about the order of the texts (#15 seems earlier than #12; #90 uses the same clear Petrarchan structure as the much earlier sonnets; and I agree that #129 is both misaligned with #120 and probably one of the last four written). I find the overall chronology and the consensus dates convincing, however, a conclusion based less on thematic continuity, or the scholarship pursuing datable reference, than on the movement toward and away from the paradigmatic Shakespearean structure.

10. For example:

Fayre is my love, when her fayre golden heares,
With the loose wynd ye waving chance to marke:
Fayre when the rose in her red cheekes appeares,
Or in her eyes the fyre of love does sparke.
Fayre when her brest lyke a rich laden barke,
With pretious merchandize she forth doth lay;
Fayre when that cloud of pryde, which oft doth dark
Her goodly light with smiles she drives away.
But fayrest she, when so she doth display,
The gate with pearles and rubyes richly dight;
Throgh which her words so wise do make their way
To bear the message of her gentle spright.
The rest be works of natures wonderment,
But this the worke of harts astonishment.
                    (Edmund Spenser, c. 1552–99;
                    from "Amoretti," MS 1595,
                    probably composed 1592–94)

Cupid and my Campaspe played
At cards for kisses; Cupid paid.
He stakes his quiver, bow, and arrows,
His mother's doves and team of sparrows,
Loses them too; then down he throws
The coral of his lip, the rose
Growing on 's cheek (but none knows how),
With these the crystal of his brow,

> And then the dimple of his chin:
> All these did my Campaspe win.
> At last he set her both his eyes;
> She won, and Cupid blind did rise.
>   Oh Love! has she done this to thee?
>   What shall, alas, become of me?
>   (John Lyly, 1554–1606; MS dated 1632)

11. Succinct observation is not unusual in a writer's response to Letters to the Editor, but eloquence certainly is. Here is Lewontin's elaboration:

> Our susceptibility to the resonance of language itself often leads us to accept what we otherwise would not believe. Although every moral and political conviction I have speaks against it, I am nearly driven by Milton's insidious poetry to believe that it is "Better to reign in Hell than serve in Heaven." For a pedagogical Aristotle this would be a particularly fine example of an "antithesis" in the "periodic" mode dissected in Book III, Part 9: the parallel but opposing structure, "Better to . . . , than to . . . ," the contrast of functionally linked "reign" and "serve," the final antithesis of "Heaven" and "Hell," two words beginning with the same sound but with different endings. For me, however, it is an almost irresistibly seductive flight of English speech, a Siren music that can be withstood only by lashing myself to the mast of my convictions.

12. Where the hunger for a system can lead is wonderfully treated by Harriet Ritvo in *The Platypus and the Mermaid and Other Figures of the Classifying Imagination* (1997).

13. A list of fruits, for instance, is a pure form unrestricted by functional structure. The formal appetite could arrange an imagistic coherence (apple/cherry/pomegranate) or an aural one (pear/peach/plum/pomegranate/papaya)—and either, because the mind prefers coherence of any stripe, may trigger the structural imagination. Both those lists move from familiar to exotic; another might use increasing size; and even such elementary organizations as these are predictive of the work of poets, whose delight in texture spurs formal and structural impulses, reinforcing one another, to generate and shape the entries.

14. If, in the intervening years, a preponderance of something like "narrative values" (and for this Plumly was only the messenger) has

emerged in poetry writing classes, I suspect it was nourished by the fact that workshops, by their nature, tend to focus on texture, especially facing texts of formal experimentation and structural incompletion. But it is naive to suggest, as many have (see, e.g., Dana Gioia, "Can Poetry Matter," *Atlantic Monthly*, May 1991), that literary culture reflects the classroom and not the other way around.

15. In the *American Poetry Review*, Ann Lauterbach provides a similar summary of the aesthetic and political moment as prelude to an entirely different set of concerns:

> Two critical linguistic/poetic habits . . . came under intense scrutiny: the "self" . . . as assumed site of authenticity and/or authority, and conventional, normative ("transparent"), discursive narration. . . . Within this dual resistance, the lyric as a form was particularly suspect, . . . synonymous with "confessional." "Confessional" meant a close relation between a given poet's life and a poem's content, particularly when that content was invested in emotional display and catharsis. The displacements of Irony became one way for a poet to be "personal." . . . Replacing the narrating I would be a formalist investment which called attention to the opacity and materiality of language, its thingness; to the reader as a crucial site of active meaning-making, and so to a rational (e.g. theoretical) ground on or by which to build poems. Questions which . . . arise around the structure of *feeling* (connected still to the irrational), the traditional site of the lyric (after all, it originates in Sappho and Archilochos, not with the English Romantics), in relation to fears of a femininzation or trivialization (marginalization) of poetry, need to be addressed. This criticique need not devolve into simplistic categories of subject-matter. ("The Night Sky IV")

Ruthless Attention

In the August 15, 1991, issue of the *New York Review of Books*, building toward the term "romantic alchemy" with which to celebrate a particular American poet as the "voice of our times," John Bayley cites five specific achievements: use of the banal, disregard for meaning, annoyance with readers who search for a subject matter, rejection of "memorable speech," and swift casualness of composition. Poems are to be praised, in short, as "talk"—the "proper noise that a poet should make," "the natural noise of a contingent present." Thus are one poet's idiosyncrasies extracted and enlarged; thus the invitation to convention. Although I do not mean to hold John Ashbery responsible for Bayley, I do mean to call attention to the critical climate in which contemporary American poets find themselves, and to grumble against the current enthusiasm for the discursive. I'll begin with some praise of my own—for Nazim Hikmet's 1947 poem, "Since I Was Thrown Inside" (translated from the Turkish by Randy Blasing and Mutlu Konuk).

Since I was thrown inside
    the earth has gone around the sun ten times.
If you ask it:
        "Not worth mentioning—
           a microscopic span."

If you ask me:
>"Ten years of my life."

I had a pencil
>the year I was thrown inside.

I used it up after a week of writing.
If you ask it:
>"A whole lifetime."

If you ask me:
>"What's a week."

Since I've been inside
>Osman did his seven-and-a-half
>>for manslaughter and left,
>>knocked around on the outside for a while,
>>then landed back inside for smuggling,
>>served six months, and got out again;
>>yesterday we had a letter—he's married,
>>with a kid coming in the spring.

They're ten years old now
>the children who were born
>>the year I was thrown inside.

And that year's foals, shaky on their spindly long legs,
>have been wide-rumped, contented mares for some time.

But the olive seedlings are still saplings,
>still children.

New squares have opened in my far-off city
>since I was thrown inside.

And my family now lives
>in a house I haven't seen
>>on a street I don't know.

Bread was like cotton, soft and white,
>the year I was thrown inside.

Then it was rationed,
and here inside men killed each other
>over black loaves the size of fists.

Now it's free again
but dark and tasteless.

The year I was thrown inside
        the SECOND hadn't started yet.

The ovens at Dachau hadn't been lit,
nor the atom bomb dropped on Hiroshima.

Time flowed like blood from a child's slit throat.
Then that chapter was officially closed.
Now the American dollar talks of a THIRD.

Still, the day has gotten lighter
                        since I was thrown inside.
And "at the edge of darkness,
        pushing against the earth with their heavy hands,
                THEY've risen up" halfway.

Since I was thrown inside
        the earth has gone around the sun ten times.
And I repeat once more with the same passion
        what I wrote about THEM
                the year I was thrown inside:

"They who are numberless like ants in the earth,
                        fish in the sea,
                        birds in the air,
who are cowardly, brave,
                ignorant, wise,
                        and childlike,
and who destroy
        and create,
my songs tell only of their adventures."
                        And anything else,
                        such as my ten years here,
                        is just so much talk.

Marginalized as we are by the surrounding culture, and furthermore embarrassed by that culture, what contemporary Amer-

ican poet can help feeling shamed as well as stirred by Hikmet's commodious poem? Another exhibit of "the noise of our times," it has both the transparency of style that presents as idiom, as "talk," and, implicitly, the analytical intelligence championed by, among others, Robert Pinsky, in his persuasive examination of the discursive in 1976 (*The Situation of Poetry*). Hikmet wrote it, at the age of forty-five, in the Turkish prison to which he had been sentenced for twenty-five years for political activism, but we underrate his great strength as a poet if we ascribe its power merely to its historical moment; as Czesław Miłosz once commented to a young poet, "You American poets envy the humpback his hump." Rather, the Hikmet poem can, I believe, serve as a model, and a tonic against convention, by recalling us to what has always lain at the center of the lyric project.

I'll point to that center by juxtaposing the Hikmet poem with its apparent opposite: a superb example of lyric compression, what his biographer calls "the last serious lines" John Keats wrote:

> This living hand, now warm and capable
> Of earnest grasping, would, if it were cold
> And in the icy silence of the tomb,
> So haunt thy days and chill thy dreaming nights
> That thou wouldst wish thine own heart dry of blood
> So in my veins red life might stream again,
> And thou be conscience-calm'd—see here it is—
> I hold it towards you.

The circumstances of that writing were as dreadful as Hikmet's. Found among the manuscript pages of "The Cap and Bells," the piece has been dated after "To Autumn" and the letter detailing his consumptive's diet of milk and vegetables: in other words, in full knowledge of his mortal illness. Certainly, Keats risks the kind of gothic vision elided by Hikmet's understatement. But his poem, like Hikmet's, does not rest on its extremity; the lines we connect in hindsight with the biographical condition follow the conditional verb (*would*) and are relegated to a qualifying, dependent clause by the IF—a clause of no greater length than the initial description of the live hand. This subordination of the dire fact is like Hikmet's choice not to use the word "prison": by the time we understand the actual dramatic situation, the tone has been established, and our automatic responses to another's imprisonment or illness—relief it's not us, and pity for the victim—have been suppressed.

What usually survives in translation is structure if not, dependably, tone. Blasing and Konuk's Hikmet, like Keats, avoids both linear narration and meditation, which necessarily concentrate material around or filter it through a protagonist. Keats relies on synecdoche (the part for the whole) to undercut further the speaker's centrality; Hikmet, on refrain: "Since I was thrown inside" and "the year I was thrown inside" become the stable, recurrent elements, functioning much as a rhymed stanzaic structure might to create "rooms" in the poem. What populates most of the rooms? Osman, children, horses, trees, the city, his family, the ovens at Dachau and the bomb at Hiroshima, world war and the threat of war, revolution, the movement of planets, ants, fish, birds—this is the world OUTSIDE, not INSIDE. Inside, a pencil, black loaves of tasteless bread, and the understated refrain—always in subordinate syntax (introductory dependent clause or adverbial phrase). This is one reason why the poem is both intensely moving and free of self-aggrandizement—but not the only reason. What Hikmet resists is the easy division that would make INSIDE hell and OUTSIDE paradise. Look at the little condensed narrative early on:

> Osman did his seven-and-a-half
>   for manslaughter and left,
>   knocked around on the outside for a while,
>   then landed back inside for smuggling,
>   served six months, and got out again;
>   yesterday we had a letter—he's married,
>   with a kid coming in the spring.

In other words, his increased mobility brings Osman only what Nadezhda Mandelstam called "ordinary heartbreak." The children are left uncharacterized except as older; the horses are well fed but nonheroic; the family merely *lives*. Outside has seen genocide, world war; THEY*'ve risen up* only halfway, who are also cowardly, ignorant, and destructive. Outside is where *Time flowed like blood from a child's slit throat*. And inside? One uses up a pencil, gets a letter, eats bread, sometimes kills for it, writes songs. Despite the difference in circumstance between the speaker and the world, there seems no difference in attention: which is to say, no special claim. The poet, Osman, the children, the mares—all are contained within the frame established by the refrain of lines 2 and 55, the *microscopic span* of ten years in which occur the epic adventures of those as numberless as ants, fish, or birds. The speaker's own lifetime falls somewhere in the middle of the spectrum, between the olive trees and the pencil.

The Keats poem, too, has no hierarchy of wretchedness. The hand is, to begin with, not characterized: not this slender hand, this familiar hand, this precious hand—not even MY hand—but merely *living, warm*; *capable* is as far as he will go to endear us, pulling back immediately—*capable of earnest grasping*. Instead of identifying with the obsessed speaker—the prerequisite to sympathy—we back away. The Other in the poem provides no comfortable point of identification either. If Hikmet resists saying "poor me," he also resists "poor you," which denies sentimentality any admittance. And Keats the same: before we can attach a body to the hand, it turns into a ghoul and a bully. Nor when the poet appears in person at the end of the poem will he relent; *see here it is— / I hold it towards you*, as if to thrust into our faces some rare, grotesque insect. Keats's speaker is one of those unwashed truth-tellers who crash the party; his refusal to charm us is total, and although attention may be commanded, pity cannot. The Hikmet poem more subtly but likewise discomforts the reader—what we expected to feel was a superiority of the "I had no shoes / he had no feet" variety.

Much has been made of Keats's ideal of "disinterestedness," a term he took from William Hazlitt and developed into "negative capability," which combines selflessness with moral imagination and which German philosophy would confirm as "empathy." None of these terms, however, with their suggestions of freedom from the self, accounts for the fierceness these two poems have in common, one of them containing multitudes—animal and vegetable life, earth and sun—the other a population of one and a hand, conditionally dead. What is notable in both is not an absence or a neutrality but something active, assertive, in the point of view, a determined and thorough attention to whatever falls within the gaze. The specimen Keats examines only happens to have grown at the end of his own arm.

I mean to identify tone or temperament, although these may be its manifestations, less than a kind of ruthless attention, an avid resolve to turn over every rock. It does not preclude the personal narrative, or even the discursive poem, but is, I believe, what can prevent such poems from dwindling into talk. Primarily I refer to the use it makes of the lyric point of view; although it does not legislate against the first-person pronoun, in its presence the experience of the poet—biographical, emotional, intellectual—becomes only another of the phenomena crowding around him or her, neither more nor less charged than any other although a great deal closer to hand, so that the poet seems, as in Robert Hass's observation about James Wright, to be writing more FROM personal experience than ABOUT such experience. Like disinterestedness, this relationship to one's material presumes that significance lies in the world, not in the poet's will to create it, and is naturally aligned with paradox and irony. Among contemporary poets it seems more common in those of damaged ego, for whom "empathy" becomes unmanageable sentiment, and it undermines, with regularity, the politically correct and the conventional.

For Philip Larkin, the convention combined lyric privilege and high rhetoric. In a preface to the 1966 reissue of *The North Ship* (1945), his first full collection, Larkin reviewed his early work:

The predominance of Yeats in this volume deserves some explanation. In 1943 the English Club was visited by Vernon Watkins; . . . impassioned and imperative, he swamped us with Yeats[,] . . . [then] distributed the volumes he had been quoting from among those of us who were nearest to him, and disappeared, exalted, into the blackout.

As a result I spent the next three years trying to write like Yeats, not because I liked his personality or understood his ideas but out of infatuation with his music. . . . In fairness to myself it must be admitted that it is a particularly potent music, pervasive as garlic, and has ruined many a better talent.

In fairness it must also be admitted that Larkin was only twenty-one years old at the time. Here are two stanzas, as demonstration:

'All men live in suffering,
I know as few can know,
Whether they take the upper road
Or stay content on the low,
Rower bent in his row-boat
Or weaver bent at his loom,
Horseman erect upon horseback
Or child hid in the womb.'

Daybreak and a candle-end.

Let the wheel spin out,
Till all created things
With shout and answering shout
Cast off rememberings;
Let it all come about
Till centuries of springs
And all their buried men
Stand on the earth again.

A drum taps: a wintry drum.

The first stanza is Yeats; the second is Larkin, in 1944, playing Yeats's drum. There were other echoes: Auden, who was acknowledged in the 1966 preface, and Housman, who was not. Yeats, however, was the permeating influence, in subject and image and sound. Larkin was careful to say he understood nothing of Yeats's "ideas" at the time, but the vastly differing musics of Mozart and Schumann, or of Yeats and Hardy, arise directly from vastly differing aesthetic "ideas" about music. I suspect he meant that he assumed the "noise of his times" without much scrutiny of it.

Hard on the heels of his first book, in 1947 Larkin assembled (but did not publish) a typescript, "In the Grip of Light," and the grip of the borrowed was still strong. "Plymouth" (written in June 1945) is typical. Totems, mementos (two boxes, a spyglass, a coin—*Last kingdom of a gold forgotten face*) open the poem but are quickly scrubbed of what Yeats called "accidence" and, by stanza 2, set free. *If they had any roughness, any flaw, / An unfamiliar scent, all this has gone,* like the golden bird in "Sailing to Byzantium" which transcends the heart, "sick with desire," and the dying animal it is fastened to, that "tattered coat upon a stick." The final stanza is enough to recall the received diction, image, and program:

> The hands that chose them rust upon a stick.
> Let my hands find such symbols, that can be
> Unnoticed in the casual light of day,
> Lying in wait for half a century
> To split chance lives across, that had not dreamed
> Such coasts had echoed, or such seabirds screamed.

Without undertaking a review of the Symbolist and Modernist agendas, I'll simply put beside that piece an unpublished, uncollected poem written almost three years later (April 1948), given momentarily without its last line:

> An April Sunday brings the snow
> Making the blossom on the plum trees green,
> Not white. An hour or two, and it will go.
> Strange that I spend that hour moving between

Cupboard and cupboard, shifting the store
Of jam you made of fruit from these same trees:
Five loads—a hundred pounds or more—
More than enough for all next summer's teas,

Which now you will not sit and eat.
Behind the glass, under the cellophane,
Remains your final summer—sweet . . .

The speaker here seems nothing BUT "a bundle of accidents"—
the same man who sits down to breakfast speaks the poem. There
is still a high interest in symbol, but the one chosen is quite easily noticed "in the casual light of day" and functions in the poem
not to trigger some vision of remote, heroic landscape but to
record an ordinary human experience: loss of a friend. And the
many textual differences between the two early Larkin pieces—
in diction, tone, music—can be seen in the aggregate as a difference in aesthetic.

Two intervening poems in the typescript date the change
more exactly. "Two Guitar Pieces," completed on September 18,
1946, merely swaps conventions: for the elevated Yeatsian sensibility, an attempt to write as an ordinary depressive at civilization's end.

I roll a cigarette, and light
A spill at the stove. With a lungful of smoke
I join you at the window that has no curtain;
There we lean on the frame, and look
Below at the platz. A man is walking along
A path between the wreckage. And we stare at the dusk,
Sharing the cigarette.
                    Behind us, our friend
Yawns, and collects the cards. The pack is short. . . .

Larkin gets right T. S. Eliot's anomie, but something else is
missing—some shame, perhaps, beneath the flat surface, something unspeakable. Eight days later, however, he writes a new

poem—one of only two he would transfer to *The Less Deceived* (1955)—and places it first in the typescript he would abandon:

> The wind blew all my wedding-day,
> And my wedding-night was the night of the high wind;
> And a stable door was banging, again and again,
> That he must go and shut it, leaving me
> Stupid in candlelight, hearing rain,
> Seeing my face in the twisted candlestick,
> Yet seeing nothing. When he came back
> He said the horses were restless, and I was sad
> That any man or beast that night should lack
> The happiness I had.
>
> (From "A Wedding-Wind")

This opening stanza with its colloquial rural persona clearly indicates some new project. Larkin had a new poetic model, named in the 1966 preface:

> When reaction came, it was undramatic, complete and permanent. In early 1946 I had some new digs in which the bedroom faced east, so that the sun woke me inconveniently early. I used to read. One book I had at my bedside was the little blue *Chosen Poems of Thomas Hardy*: Hardy I knew as a novelist, but as regards his verse I shared Lytton Strachey's verdict that "the gloom is not even relieved by a little elegance of diction." This opinion did not last long.

One passage from Hardy can serve as illustration:

> "I shot him dead because—
> Because he was my foe,
> Just so: my foe of course he was;
> That's clear enough; although
>
> "He'd thought he'd 'list, perhaps,
> Off-hand like—just as I—

Was out of work—had sold his traps—
  No other reason why.

"Yes; quaint and curious war is!
  You shoot a fellow down
You'd treat if met where any bar is,
  Or help to half-a-crown."
         (From "The Man He Killed")

Hardy offered exactly the permission, and the leverage, Larkin needed. Whereas Yeats's elegant abstractions and imagery labor to make of his fisherman, his airman, his Irish martyrs figures of resonance and significance ("A lonely impulse of delight / Drove to this tumult in the clouds . . ."), in Hardy the craft is employed in observation and precise rendering.

In his *Paris Review* interview in 1982, Larkin said about early influences:

> What effects? Yeats and Auden, the management of lines, the formal distancing of emotion. Hardy, well . . . not to be afraid of the obvious. All those wonderful *dicta* about poetry: "the poet should touch our hearts by showing his own," "the poet takes note of nothing that he cannot feel," "the emotion of all the ages and the thought of his own"—Hardy knew what it was all about. (*Required Writing*)

"An April Sunday" also makes clear that the new influence affected more than his music. First, there is a shift in subject matter from the sublime to the quotidian, and with it a shift from high style into low. Second, a complication of persona and pronouns, not merely a conversion of the poet's own experience into second or third person but the poet's undertaking of other kinds of experience, an effort natural enough for a novelist but in less general practice among poets. Third, a reliance on both tonal and dramatic irony, often sacrificing the dignity of the speaker for the sake of representative characterization. And fourth—my primary interest here—concern with perception more than with utterance. It is partly this last that leads Larkin to distinguish Yeats's impassioned lines as "distanced," reserving "feeling" for something less grand, something obvious and democratized. In *Required Writing*, Larkin describes his source:

> [W]hat I like about [Hardy] primarily is his temperament and the way he sees life. He's not a transcendental writer, he's not a Yeats, he's not an Eliot; his subjects are men, the life of men, time and the passing of time, love and the fading of love. When I came to Hardy it was with the sense of relief that I didn't have to try and jack myself up to a concept of poetry that lay outside my own life—this is perhaps what I felt Yeats was trying to make me do. One could simply relapse back into one's own life and write from it. Hardy taught one to feel rather than to write—of course one has to use one's own language and one's own jargon and one's own situations—and he taught one as well to have confidence in what one felt. . . . I think Hardy's diction is often quaint . . . but I feel that the quaintness . . . is a kind of striving to be accurate.

"An April Sunday" was written in 1948, the year that Larkin turned twenty-six, Eliot won the Nobel (five years after publication of *The Four Quartets*), Pound published the Pisan Cantos, and Yeats's body was exhumed and brought back to Sligo. The poem is heavily figured, but the symbol seems chosen for, not released from, its *roughness*, *flaw*, and *scent*. Instead of ecstatic vision or earnest wishing for it, we are given irony, overt, heavy-handed, and Hardyesque: snow (death) shows the white blossoms for what they actually are (green—that is, young, alive); the snow lasts only an hour, whereas the trees have an annual renewable "life"; the "you" doesn't get to enjoy the "fruits" of her labor. Instead of sonority the poem's first fidelity is to idiom, and it strains for casual speech, just as early poems strained for high rhetoric, with lines either padded or broken awkwardly across the metered line and the rhymed stanza. There is some unease, too, around the blunt analogue of jam and the dead one's *final summer*. The poem risks sentiment, as Hardy does, in the main character, here given nothing to do but register the parallels and enact the torpor of grief, *moving between / Cupboard and cupboard.* A different music, a different aesthetic: Larkin's speaker is now less the poet who knows "as few can know," as Yeats had it, than the reader's representative.

The lyric strategy in this poem perhaps seems familiar to us by now: an initial nod to the natural world, establishing the speaker as a fellow of sensitivity and modesty; a domestic action, initially innocuous but revealed to be Significant and Resonant; and then the epiphany. A student poet might finish it:

Behind the glass, under the cellophane,
Remains your final summer—sweet
And clear. I dip my spoon again.

Or, from the School of Anguish:

Behind the glass, under the cellophane,
Remains your final summer—sweet,
Sweet loss. I lift the lid on pain.

Larkin's closing insight is less conventional and less precious. There is a clue in that opening observation (*Making the blossom on the plum trees green, / Not white*), an exactitude about the blossoms that seems almost petulant, grudging, rendered as it is primarily by negation. Here is Larkin's ending:

Strange that I spend that hour moving between

Cupboard and cupboard, shifting the store
Of jam you made of fruit from these same trees:
Five loads—a hundred pounds or more—
More than enough for all next summer's teas,

Which now you will not sit and eat.

Behind the glass, under the cellophane,
Remains your final summer—sweet
And meaningless, and not to come again.

Hardy's influence on Larkin was permanent and enabling, and one can trace it through the frequency of dialogue, local character, and bitter humor in Larkin's published and unpublished poems. But to do so perhaps traces limitation, since Larkin at his most Hardyesque sometimes gets mired in the anachronistic, regional, or reductively ironic. Finally, to substitute one great writer's shadow for another's is to continue writing in the comfortable shade. What interests us is the deeper lesson for Larkin: "One could simply relapse back into one's own life and write from it." One's own life, however, is a complex and sometimes triangulated matter.

On January 3, 1950, Larkin wrote the first poem of his first mature volume, *The Less Deceived*, and six weeks later composed the poem that would supply the book's title:

Deceptions

'Of course I was drugged, and so heavily I did not regain my consciousness till the next morning. I was horrified to discover that I had been ruined, and for some days I was inconsolable, and cried like a child to be killed or sent back to my aunt.' Mayhew, *London Labour And The London Poor*

Even so distant, I can taste the grief,
Bitter and sharp with stalks, he made you gulp.
The sun's occasional print, the brisk brief
Worry of wheels along the street outside
Where bridal London bows the other way,
And light, unanswerable and tall and wide,
Forbids the scar to heal, and drives
Shame out of hiding. All the unhurried day
Your mind lay open like a drawer of knives.

Slums, years, have buried you. I would not dare
Console you if I could. What could be said,
Except that suffering is exact, but where
Desire takes charge, readings will grow erratic?
For you would hardly care
That you were less deceived, out on that bed,
Than he was, stumbling up the breathless stair
To burst into fulfilment's desolate attic.

"Deceptions" shows that Larkin's apprenticeship was not entirely outgrown: he had learned from Auden's "abject willow" to displace human emotion onto a neutral narrative detail and gives us two of these displacements in the last two lines (*breathless stair* and *desolate attic*); line 6 uses the series of three (*unanswerable and tall and wide*, like Yeats's "Colder and dumber and deafer than a fish") sacrificed by Yeats in a later, tougher syntax and kept as a Larkin trademark; and the headnote's prose account offers Hardyesque character and event. But there are also three indicators of mature, characteristic Larkin and the point-of-view advantage I mean to isolate.

First, as is true of "An April Sunday," "Two Guitar Pieces," and "A Wedding-Wind," the dramatic occasion has not been shorn from the poem but left intact and developed with both the headnote and the active description in the first stanza. If the opening two lines seem pushy in their claim (*I can taste the grief . . . he made you gulp*), nevertheless the energy of language, figure, and music in the second sentence marks imaginative and moral involvement in the experience of another, much like what we saw in Hikmet's delineation of the "outside."

Second, figuration and statement address feeling, even if somewhat clumsily. Grief is *bitter and sharp with stalks*; shame wants to cringe in the shadows. The initial detail in "An April Sunday" (snow making *the blossom on the plum trees green, / Not white*) supplied a visual phenomenon made applicable to human predicament by the poet's inclusion of it, its conjunction with elegy; here, each stanza ends in a dramatic image, a concrete embodiment of complex emotions. The first of these, *Your mind lay open like a drawer of knives*, compels at least in part because it tries so hard, suggesting simultaneously choice of weapons and innocent household clutter. Likewise, while his *stumbling up the breathless stair / To burst into fulfilment's desolate attic* is the sexiest passage in the poem, the restored adjective/noun pairing links it to the *brisk . . . worry of wheels* in get-ahead London.

Third, we notice the speaker's determination to examine all related phenomena: that the sun and the wheels are *occasional, brisk,* and *brief* in contrast to the victim's permanent scar; that although *suffering is exact,* perception of it is not; that despite her anguish, or because of it, the victim is *less deceived, out on that bed,* than the attacker; that she *would hardly care* that this is the case, though clearly the poet does. And we register his fierce concentration on the reconstructed scene as the poem tips itself toward chaos at its closure. The first stanza is dominated by lovely, orderly tercets—*grief/gulp/brief, outside/way/wide, drives/day/knives*—in masculine full rhyme, with the second set yoked both discreetly (*wide/drives*) and overtly (*way/day*) to the third, recalling (the binary form prods us) a sonnet's closely unified octave. Despite the dropped foot in line 7, the iambic pentameter is steady. Stanza 2 seems to continue the formal pattern but slips instead into an extended alternating rhyme (*dare/said/where/erratic/care*), returning in line 15 to chime the stanza's second sound (*said/bed*): the recurrent sounds are there but not in the established pattern. What might have been the *a* rhyme of the second tercet—*erratic,* with its surprising final unstressed syllable, put further off balance by the question mark and the three-beat line that follows—is left unpaired until the very last line, where the double rhyme (*erratic/attic*) ends the iambic poem on a falling rhythm. Once it's past us, we see that the stanza is not the interlocked tercets we expected but duplicated quatrains. This is clearly a poet fearless of contradiction and paradox.

Vernon Watkins reappeared ten years after their first encounter, only now the debate "was Hardy versus Yeats. . . . I had settled into a poetic tradition very different from Vernon's, and found much of what he said unacceptable." What was "unacceptable," one can assume, was having "to try and jack myself up to a concept of poetry that lay outside my own life," as he would later describe his early work. Nor, however, could he write comfortably ABOUT himself—there are few biographical clues in his work, beyond geography and class—an impediment of great consequence to the lyric project of writing about feelings, since one's own feelings provide the primary, most reliable, case studies. The solution lay in point of view: Larkin held a lens to ordinary experience (read, HIS experience, if you like) and looked through it without censure or predisposition.

"Deceptions" shows us one outcome: the admitted marginality of the self, the observing sensibility. Here, the poet/speaker appears only as part of the dramatic frame—unidentified man, reading another person's testimony, whose response to the central events is both recorded and dismissed (*For you would hardly care*). That this rejection of lyric privilege was the beginning of mature, characteristic work can be shown by the arc between "Deceptions" (1950) and his last major poem—I would say his greatest poem, as well—"The Old Fools" (1973). We can graph the progress briefly with one poem from each of his remaining volumes: "Talking In Bed" (1960) from *The Whitsun Weddings*, and "Sad Steps" (1968) from *High Windows*.

If in "Deceptions" the speaker is peripheral, in "Talking in Bed" (1960) he is subsumed into anonymous, or entirely representative, experience.

> Talking in bed ought to be easiest,
> Lying together there goes back so far,
> An emblem of two people being honest.
>
> Yet more and more time passes silently.
> Outside, the wind's incomplete unrest
> Builds and disperses clouds about the sky,
>
> And dark towns heap upon the horizon.

> None of this cares for us. Nothing shows why
> At this unique distance from isolation
>
> It becomes still more difficult to find
> Words at once true and kind,
> Or not untrue and not unkind.

No personal pronoun appears at all until line 8, and there not the subject of a sentence but the object of a preposition (*None of this cares for us*). Plural, it may be read narrowly, "two people being honest," or broadly—all of "us," with the autobiographical poet left as sketchy, as removed from the actual dramatic occasion as he was in "Deceptions." The grounding of occasion is still present, though done more deftly, more economically, than in the earlier poem: two people talking in bed, finding less and less to say, the silence filling with the sound of the wind outside. The poem's one sustained image again centers on feeling, on common or ordinary emotional experience, but it works through negation, first projecting onto the natural world (*the wind's incomplete unrest / Builds and disperses clouds about the sky*), then exaggerating, distorting, nature's sympathetic role (*dark towns heap up on the horizon*) before its claim is undermined by statement. Straightaway then to the end, the poet admits having no special insight:

> None of this cares for us. Nothing shows why
> At this unique distance from isolation
>
> It becomes still more difficult to find
> Words at once true and kind,
> Or not untrue and not unkind.

But this is, in poet/critic Susan Stewart's vocabulary, a poem of discovery and not complaint. As readers, we are persuaded of the discovery—that it IS more difficult—because of the same effort at precise calibration that marked phrases like *green, not white* and *less deceived* in the earlier poems, reinforced here by the formal authority of the final tercet. After all that graceful, idiomatic iambic pentameter, after three tercets, a shadow of terza rima falling over them (*easiest/far/honest, silently/unrest/sky, horizon/ why/isolation*), we find ourselves with a pure triplet (*find/kind/ unkind*), the last rhyme an exact repetition, the last two lines also rhymed internally (*true and kind/untrue and unkind*) and fore-shortened into tetrameter to better serve the final modification— all of which focuses the mind on the double negatives and the prefix appearing for the second and third time in the poem: *un-*. Such exactitude of feeling and predicament seems to me at least less probable in discursive poems that have relaxed the formal, economical, musical context in which intricate distinctions like these can register.

What, then, about direct personal narrative, where the cam-era angle is secured within—and revelatory of—the poet-as-protagonist? It's not simply a matter of first-person pronoun, as can be made obvious by inserting pronouns where Larkin omitted them:

> Talking [to you] in bed ought to be easiest,
> [Our] lying together there goes back so far . . .

Immediately, the next line, *An emblem of two people being hon-est*, is rendered implausible and pretentious and the poem's final sentence unimaginable. In Larkin, as in Keats and Hikmet, when a seemingly autobiographical speaker does put in an appearance, he gets no special favors.

Sad Steps

> Groping back to bed after a piss
> I part thick curtains, and am startled by
> The rapid clouds, the moon's cleanliness.
>
> Four o'clock: wedge-shadowed gardens lie
> Under a cavernous, a wind-picked sky.
> There's something laughable about this,

The way the moon dashes through clouds that blow
Loosely as cannon-smoke to stand apart
(Stone-coloured light sharpening the roofs below)

High and preposterous and separate—
Lozenge of love! Medallion of art!
O wolves of memory! Immensements! No,

One shivers slightly, looking up there.
The hardness and the brightness and the plain
Far-reaching singleness of that wide stare

Is a reminder of the strength and pain
Of being young; that it can't come again,
But is for others undiminished somewhere.

                                                April 1968

In the Sidney sonnet to which Larkin alludes ("With how sad
steps, Oh Moon, thou climb'st the skies"), the moon is companionable, a fellow sufferer of love. Here, like Hikmet's planetary
revolutions, though less stable, the moon keeps the first-person
pronoun in proper (diminished) proportion, providing a large,
continuing perspective by which any particular human distress—
the poet's own most especially—must be measured. At the same
time, notice how myopic the poet is, how scrupulously detailed—
wedge-shadowed gardens; *a cavernous, a wind-picked sky*; *clouds
that blow / Loosely as cannon-smoke*; *Stone-coloured light sharpening the roofs below*. This fabric of unstinting precision makes
obvious, in diction and syntax, when the moon is obscured or altered, not only by clouds but by the protagonist's own romanticizing sensibility:

High and preposterous and separate—
Lozenge of love! Medallion of art!
O wolves of memory! Immensements! No . . .

What immeasurable effect on tone has been made with the introduction of the slant rhyme and accumulating caesuras! De-

spite its usual aggrandizing, or because aggrandizement is admitted to the poem and deflated, establishing aggressive equality between one individual's experience and the world's, the first-person pronoun here is only a step away from the inclusive plurals of "The Old Fools."

"Deceptions," "Talking in Bed," and "Sad Steps" examine complicated emotional predicaments along a chronological spectrum of decreasing authorial distance from the material. The collapsing distance (which is to say, increasing dramatic centrality of the point of view) is less interesting, however, than the concomitant DECREASE in overt sympathy for the protagonist: the closer to the dramatic center, the more ruthlessly is the point-of-view sensibility itself examined. One might think the correlation only part of Larkin's famously bitchy defense of privacy, were it not for the compositional record of "The Old Fools" (January 1973), suggested, in lieu of available drafts, by *The Collected Poems*.

"Heads in the Women's Ward" (May 1972), like "The View" (August 1972), was deservedly omitted from *High Windows* (1974), his last volume, and is notable only in its coupling of Larkin's obsessive subject and a particular interest in the physical record: *Jaws stand open; necks are stretched / With every tendon sharply sketched*. What sinks it is the point of view, a determinedly absent omniscient speaker, which summarizes and then abandons the poem to a sentimental heap of nouns:

> Sixty years ago they smiled
> At lover, husband, first-born child.

> Smiles are for youth. For old age come
> Death's terror and delirium.

On the other hand, in "The View" the speaker/poet is the insider, content with an amalgam of languid statements, a willingness to generalize, and a residue of popular idiom. It is largely rhymed talk, one might say uncharitably, and the rhymes are achieved without subtlety:

The view is fine from fifty,
    Experienced climbers say;
So, overweight and shifty,
    I turn to face the way
    That led me to this day.

In the last stanza, his famous negatives (*unchilded and unwifed*)
are dragged in and left unexplored: mannerism. If "Heads in the
Women's Ward" stays outside the emotional experience, "The
View" seems simply self.

Yet here is the central metaphor for the poem that marks the
pinnacle and end of Larkin's major work. Although merely formal
occasion and emblem of the poet's dilemma in "The View," it will
recur in the next poem of record (five months later) with characteristic precision of detail, ruthless insight, energized negatives,
and surprising pronouns. "The Old Fools" doesn't turn from but
faces and names the end of the climb:

What do they think has happened, the old fools,
To make them like this? Do they somehow suppose
It's more grown-up when your mouth hangs open and drools,
And you keep on pissing yourself, and can't remember
Who called this morning? Or that, if they only chose,
They could alter things back to when they danced all night,
Or went to their wedding, or sloped arms some September?
Or do they fancy there's really been no change,
And they've always behaved as if they were crippled or tight,
Or sat through days of thin continuous dreaming
Watching light move? If they don't (and they can't), it's
    strange:
                            Why aren't they screaming?

Like the difference between *wild white hair and staring eyes* (in
"Heads in the Women's Ward") and *Ash hair, toad hands, prune
face dried into lines* in the next stanza of "The Old Fools," what
distinguishes the poem immediately from its two failed prede-
cessors is its tone of outraged witness. And even that much dis-

tance is stripped away as the poem drives through the stanzas; what could be more opposite to the chatty diffidence of "The View" (*Where has it gone, the lifetime?* / *Search me*) than this:

> Perhaps being old is having lighted rooms
> Inside your head, and people in them, acting.
> People you know, yet can't quite name; each looms
> Like a deep loss restored, from known doors turning.
> Setting down a lamp, smiling from a stair, extracting
> A known book from the shelves; or sometimes only
> The rooms themselves, chairs and a fire burning,
> The blown bush at the window, or the sun's
> Faint friendliness on the wall some lonely
> Rain-ceased midsummer evening. That is where they live:
> Not here and now, but where all happened once.

Meanwhile, as the pronouns shifting between third and second person lead us toward the final complicitous *we*, the participant point of view made explicit, the figure salvaged from "The View" enlarges and adjusts the scale of imagery and action, much like Hikmet's revolving sun:

> This is why they give

> An air of baffled absence, trying to be there
> Yet being here. For the rooms grow farther, leaving
> Incompetent cold, the constant wear and tear
> Of taken breath, and them crouching below
> Extinction's alp, the old fools, never perceiving
> How near it is. This must be what keeps them quiet:
> The peak that stays in view wherever we go
> For them is rising ground. Can they never tell
> What is dragging them back, and how it will end? Not at
>   night?
> Not when the strangers come? Never, throughout
> The whole hideous inverted childhood? Well,
>   We shall find out.

In our "contingent present," the examination of strong feeling seems to have become either suspect or irrelevant. Certainly, the revival of the discursive mode developed in part in reaction against a dead-ended Confessionalism—even though, like many such revolts, it contains what it overthrows in its presumption that experience coheres only in the poet's utterance of it. But perhaps the emotional life is finally all that connects us, one to another, in what used to be called the human condition, and even banal subjects (talking in bed, taking a piss) may become memorable speech in a musical context. For those who still hold this old-fashioned view, which stands at the heart of the lyric project, what Larkin affirms for us—what Hardy affirmed for Larkin—is that great poems require neither the extraordinary life circumstances of Keats or Hikmet nor Bayley's "romantic alchemy" but a relentless "striving to be accurate" and, sometimes, a certain ruthlessness toward the very sensibility that produces the poem.

A Moment's Thought

... a line will take us hours maybe;
Yet if it does not seem a moment's thought,
Our stitching and unstitching has been naught.
—W. B. Yeats, "Adam's Curse"

In *Dr. Zhivago* (the movie) there is a scene in which handsome, mustached Omar Sharif, surrogate for Boris Pasternak, bundled up against the dangerous cold in his empty dacha with Julie Christie and Geraldine Chaplin relegated off-screen, is composing a love poem. While the theme song strums softly in the background, the camera pans the vast snow-blown, wolf-haunted steppes, moving in slowly to show the poet sitting alone in a large room at a low table, alternately staring out the window and bending down to his heavy-weight bond paper. He pauses, chews his pen, adjusts his ragged gloves and long scarf, then balls the paper into a wad and throws it to the floor. Music swells. The candle flickers (surely there was a candle). He starts again, muttering under his visible breath; he scratches a line, sighs, again wads and chucks it. Camera cuts to the wolves (passing of time), within yards of the house by now, returns to the brow-furrowed poet, his feet in drifts of discarded drafts as if in snow. Finally, Omar gazes upward, music grows louder, the mustache curves into a smile, the orthodontically ideal teeth sparkle.

Closeup of his hand: the pen is suddenly moving fluently over the page, supplying the rhymed and metered lines of the completed poem.

Don't blame Hollywood: it is a received image of long standing, as is this perennial from the Q-and-A after a reading: "Where do you get your ideas?" What's unimaginable is DOING THE THING AT ALL. The public believes that a novel requires only a few months off from work and a used Underwood typewriter, but poems lurk in the shallows, occluded but whole, needing the right bait and a little luck. Except we don't call it luck; we call it "inspiration," and whether they've seen the movie or not, this image of themselves is where most young poets begin—though without the wolves, without the violins, and too often without the debris of false starts, botched drafts.

Not that it NEVER happens that way; poets, like athletes, sometimes find "the zone" where every shot swishes through the basket (though seldom in rhymed pentameter)—usually during a period of fluency in a new, newly comfortable mode. But it is a tyrannical model. Notice, in the more sophisticated original, articulated in 1800 by William Wordsworth in his preface to the *Lyrical Ballads*, the aggressive modifier: "For *all* good poetry is the spontaneous overflow of powerful feelings" (my italics). Of course, as with blurbs that retain the desirable adjective and suppress the otherwise negative review, Wordsworth's full sentence is often left unquoted:

> For all good poetry is the spontaneous overflow of powerful feelings; and though this be true, Poems to which any value can be attached were never produced on any variety of subjects but by a man who, being possessed of more than usual organic sensibility, had also thought long and deeply.

There they are, the Scylla and Charybdis of the art: the special gift and the elusiveness of its fruition; "more than usual organic sensibility" and long deep thought; or, in the American adaptation, eyes to the ceiling and wads of white paper on the floor.

Even in cliché, as in the original, the formulation nods to paradox: that a poem derives from both receptivity and active will, that it requires both imagination and technique. Two muses, then—or Nietzsche's two gods of art, an id and a superego: Dionysus, God of wine and orgy, of feeling and flow and spontaneity; and Apollo, stern God of light, order, balance, the cognitive mind. The danger, and not just for beginning poets, is that in profile they seem all too much like handsome, exuberant youth on the one hand, and cautious, pedestrian middle age on the other. And that's been enough to give revision a bad reputation, odor of the clerk, the drudge, and the nerd.

The bias was there from the start, in Wordsworth's call for an organic poetry, one disassociated from philosophy and realigned with the mystics.

I have said that poetry is the spontaneous overflow of powerful feelings: it takes its origin from emotion recollected in tranquility; the emotion is contemplated till, by a species of reaction, the tranquility gradually disappears, and an emotion, kindred to that which was before the subject of contemplation is gradually produced, and does itself actually exist in the mind. In this mood successful composition generally begins, and in a mood similar to this it is carried on.

Elsewhere in his preface Wordsworth defines "this mood" as a "state of excitement," about which he adds, "ideas and feelings do not, in that state, succeed each other in accustomed order"—allowing Apollo at least into the theater. But the stage directions for Omar Sharif are clear: emotion is both wellspring and bucket, lens and subject; the poet is to be transported.

Meanwhile, there has appeared, since Wordsworth, another formulation, redistributing the weight: Einstein's definition of genius as 10 percent inspiration, 90 percent perspiration; or Flannery O'Connor's wonderful crack that she wasn't a genius, merely talented, so she had to work very hard at her fiction. The same shift away from the primacy of the natural and the received underlies Eliot's regard for the Metaphysical poets' passionate *thought*, the New Critical attention to irony, paradox, figure, and wit, and Yeats's cautionary

> Better go down upon your marrow-bones
> And scrub a kitchen pavement, or break stones
> Like an old pauper, in all kinds of weather;
> For to articulate sweet sounds together
> Is to work harder than all these.
>
> ("Adam's Curse")

This is, of course, still the Orphic ideal, poet as special case, a "more than usual organic sensibility," but the High Modernists (although their adjective might have been "erudite" rather than "organic") focused on the gap between that sensibility and the page. Pound's definition of image, his insistence on poetry at least as well written as prose, his skill as an editor, and his "Ezuversity" restored both educated intelligence and a work ethic to the notion of what a poet actually does. For a model we might take the figure of Hemingway, doggedly writing his requisite number of paragraphs every day; or Dylan Thomas when sober—hours taking out a comma, hours putting it back.

In Yeats's case, many of his poems are first signaled in manuscript by a prose note sketching a subject, often followed by the end words of a rhyme scheme. (These materials are available from several sources; I'd recommend Curtis Bradford's *Yeats at Work*). For instance, this notebook entry:

> Topic for poem. School children and the thought that life will waste them, perhaps that no possible life can fulfill their own dreams or even their teacher's hope. Bring in the old thought that life prepares for what never happens.

Seeing tranquillity lowered to hypothermia, one would hardly think to ask Yeats, "Where did you get that idea?" (a topic he treated with high-class voodoo: a sudden smell of roses, voices dictating to his enrapt wife) but rather, "What happened" between the first logged source and the masterpiece, "Among School Children"? That question is answered only obliquely, in the poem's serene—one might say inspired—closure:

> O body swayed to music, O brightening glance,
> How can we know the dancer from the dance?

The important distinction between the two formulations, then, may not lie in the popular but simplistic opposition of inspiration versus labor. Seamus Heaney, in "The Makings of a Music," shrewdly maps the common ground:

I chose the word "makings" for the title because it gestures towards the testings and hesitations of the workshop, the approaches towards utterance, the discovery of lines and then the intuitive extension of the vital element in those lines over a whole passage. . . . The given line (*donné*), the phrase or cadence which haunts the ear and the eager parts of the mind, this is the tuning fork to which the whole music of the poem is orchestrated, *that out of which* the overall melodies are worked for or calculated. It is my impression that this haunting or donné *occurs to all poets in much the same way, arbitrarily*, with a sense of promise, as an alertness, a hankering, a readiness. It is also my impression that the quality of the music in the finished poem has to do with *the way the poet proceeds to respond to his donné*. If he surrenders to it, allows himself to be carried by its *initial* rhythmic suggestiveness, to become somnambulist after its *invitations*, then we will have a music not unlike Wordsworth's, hypnotic, swimming with the current of its form rather than against it. If, on the other hand, instead of surrendering to the drift of the *original, generating* rhythm, the poet seeks to discipline it, to harness its energies in order to drive other parts of his mind into motion, then we will have a music not unlike Yeats's, affirmative, seeking to master rather than to mesmerize the ear, swimming strongly against the current of its form. (*Preoccupations*; my italics)

This is beautifully written and convincing, allowing for the differences in temperament between Wordsworth's "mood" of composition and Yeats's pauper breaking stones but maintaining the primacy of a crucial generative moment. In Heaney's analysis — as, I suspect, in the self-edited memories of making our own poems — both examples, Wordsworth and Yeats, presume an INITIAL *donné*, visited upon us or sprung from the subconscious, which then is either followed or struggled against as the poet "proceeds to respond" (Heaney) in "a species of reaction" (Wordsworth). Dionysus, then Apollo; the right side of the brain, then the left; presentiment, then articulation; music, then language; Paul Valéry's *vers donné*, what is given, then *vers calculé*, what is made.

What I'd adjust in this narrative is the fixed sequence, extending Heaney's point about relatively active or passive engagement with the muse. The focused attention ("alertness") that poems require need not always occur "to all poets in much the same way, arbitrarily," but may evolve from the "habit of art" (O'Connor quoting Jacques Maritain) or a "rage for order" (Wallace Stevens); instructive cadence can follow, rather than always precede, rational application of craft; and if visitation cannot be willed, it nonetheless remains a disguised part of the will and may be willfully invited. Following the prose notes as they do, Yeats's auditions for stanza form and rhyme scheme strike me as just such an invitation, stone struck against stone until one finally sparks and a resonant organization of the material begins in that light. From there, under the litter of subsequent drafts, one can see the essential poem emerge, see the fusion of thought and feeling, music and idea — what Graham Hough calls "luminosity" — not precipitate but actually ARISE FROM prosaic calculation. Even Wordsworth allowed as much, restricting his crucial "species of reaction," in whose thrall the pen races across the page, to "a man who . . . had thought long and deeply." In the compositional mood, or state of excitement, he said, "ideas and feelings do not . . . succeed each other in accustomed order." There lies great encouragement: vision may be the fruit of technique, not only its precursor, and the *donné* need not be FIRST cause. Think of Pope's "happy coincidence in search of a rhyme"—the sheer generative power of a restrictive form. Or Keats setting out on yet another disposable sonnet, such as he and friends often penned for amusement in Leigh Hunt's parlor, but writing instead "On First Looking into Chapman's Homer."

Nevertheless—no matter the proportions, no matter the sequence—the problem with the dialectic model remains: what finally accounts for the firing across the synapse, the bridging, in communicable text, of craft and cadence, will and vision, labored-for precision and elusive grace? Well, there is this from Lewis Thomas, physician, research scientist, and wonderful essayist:

> A solitary ant, afield, cannot be considered to have much of anything on his mind; indeed, with only a few neurons strung together by fibers, he can't be imagined to have a mind at all, much less a thought. He is more like a ganglion on legs. Four ants together, or ten, encircling a dead moth on a path, begin to look more like an idea. They fumble and shove, gradually moving the food toward the Hill, but as though by blind chance. It is only when you watch the dense mass of thousands of ants, crowded together around the Hill, blackening the ground, that you begin to see the whole beast, and now you observe it thinking, planning, calculating. It is an intelligence . . . with crawling bits for its wits. ("On Societies as Organisms")

"Crawling bits"—Thomas anticipated almost entirely the latest surmises about the human brain. The recent bicameral (and thoroughly Nietzschean) model—right brain for intuition, emotion, art, and music; left brain for logic, rational thought, and language—is already outdated; such neat divisions were never verified except in pathology. In its place has come the concept of "modularity," of a lifetime of data not stored on labeled shelves in the closet but processed multiply by distinct networks of differing function: this very sentence as you read it dismantled by your brain into its component parts—one set of ganglions taking care of the nouns, another the verbs; another flashing up your own shelf, in your own closet at home, from the image depot; a separate hardwired board parsing out the syntax you may have been born to; the brain's musicians tuning up to the lexical and syntactical repetitions I'm using; and a brand new neural pathway extending itself like algae shot with Rapid-Gro to accommodate this new word "modularity" and its baggage, "modules" and "modern" and "insularity" and "modular housing" and even, from the rhyming crew, "nodules," even "noodles." Thought, it seems, is not the linear storage and retrieval system we know from computers. And if Thomas's analogy holds for the way we receive, process, and act on information, consider what must be happening when we set out to produce a poem, a complex construct made from intuition, observation, experience, erudition, music, memory, and feeling—what Coleridge called "the blossom and the fragrancy of all human knowledge, human thoughts, human passions, motions, language."

Thomas suggests a model for that as well:

> "Stigmergy" is a new word, invented recently by Grassé to explain the nest-building behavior of termites, perhaps generalizable to other complex activities of social animals. The word is made of Greek roots meaning "to incite to work," and Grassé's intention was to indicate that it is *the product of work itself that provides both the stimulus and instructions for further work* [my italics]. He arrived at this after long observation of the construction of termite nests, which excepting perhaps a man-made city are the most formidable edifices in nature. . . .
>
> The interiors of the nests are like a three-dimensional maze, intricate arrangements of spiraling galleries, corridors, and arched vaults, ventilated and air-conditioned. There are great caverns for the gardens of fungi on which the termites depend for their nourishment, perhaps also as a source of

heat. There is a rounded vaulted chamber for the queen, called the royal cell. The fundamental structural unit, on which the whole design is based, is the arch. ("Living Language")

Termites and ants, Thomas had noted in the earlier essay, are "extraordinary in the way they seem to accumulate intelligence as they gather together."

> Grassé placed a handful of termites in a dish filled with soil and fecal pellets and watched what they did. . . . [T]hey all simply ran around, picking up pellets at random and dropping them again. Then, by chance, two or three pellets happened to light on top of each other, and this transformed the behavior of everyone. Now they displayed the greatest interest and directed their attention obsessively to the primitive column, adding new pellets and fragments of earth. After reaching a certain height, the construction stopped unless another column was being formed nearby; in this case, the structure changed from a column to an arch, bending off in a smooth curve, [and] the arch was joined. ("Living Language")

Thomas had already warned us:

> It is not known how . . . the chains of termites building one column know when to turn toward the crew on the adjacent column, or how, when the time comes, they manage the flawless joining of the arches. The stimuli . . . set them off, . . . building collectively instead of shifting things about. . . . They react as if alarmed. They become agitated, excited, and then they begin working, like artists. ("On Societies as Organisms")

"The product of work itself . . . provides both the stimulus and instructions for further work." Our mistake, perhaps, has been to privilege one module over the other in our narratives of the creative process. To mythologize—externalize—discovery is to infantilize the poet; to overcultivate the will, on the other hand, is to perpetuate the conventional in form and thought, endless replicas of "Endymion" and never Keats's odes.

Consider a first extant draft (backs of envelopes, penciled napkins, or a dreamed image not having been preserved) from Elizabeth Bishop's manuscript papers, titled, successively, "How To Lose Things?" "The Gift Of Losing Things?" and "The Art Of Losing Things" (see Figure 1). The page suggests a modular mind at work: a dead moth on the path (mislaid car keys or glasses) and a solitary ant, then four ants, ten, circling it, fumbling and shoving. The bossy logical ants are busy with plans:

> One might begin . . .
> The thing to do is to begin . . .
> Mostly, one begins . . .

The tactical ants are trying out pronouns:

> One begins, one is making progress . . .
> I really want to introduce myself . . .
> You may find it hard to believe . . .
> One might think this would have prepared me . . .
> He who loseth his life, etc . . .

The ethical ants object from the sidelines:

> these are almost too easy to be mentioned . . .
> I have actually lost I mean <u>lost,</u> and forever . . .
> maybe it's lost too. I won't know for sure for some time . . .

The adolescent ants are talking back and acting out (*only the eyes* WERE *exceptionally beautiful*); the literate ants cite the Bible (*He who loseth . . .*); the sentimental ants break down and weep (*All gone, gone forever and ever*); the musical ants break into song (*and* MAny SMALLer BITS *of* geOGraphy).

Or maybe that's the wrong insect. IS there, in fact, a dead moth fortuitously on the path? Or is the absentmindedness what Richard Hugo called the false, the triggering subject, and was the poet in her long habit of composition "picking up pellets at random

Figure 1. Draft #1 of "One Art" by Elizabeth Bishop from Vassar Special Collections. Copyright © 1995 by Alice Helen Methfessel. Used by permission of the estate of Elizabeth Bishop and Farrar, Straus & Giroux, Inc. All rights reserved.

and dropping them again" until "by chance, two or three pellets happened to light on top of each other"? After the first long verse paragraph we can chart something accruing. A verb suddenly predominates—*lost / I mean LOST*—occurring in lines 1, 2, 5, 6, 7, 9. And there is other close repetition: *houses, house; island, island; small-sized, smaller; two whole cities, two of the world's biggest cities (two of the most beautiful . . .); a piece of one continent, one entire continent.* As if "the product of work itself . . . provide[d] both the stimulus and instructions for further work, . . . this transformed the behavior of everyone. Now they displayed the greatest interest and directed their attention obsessively to the primitive column, adding new pellets and fragments of earth. After reaching a certain height, the construction stopped unless another column was being formed nearby."

After a short stanza of assertion and contradiction, after picking up again the dropped stitch (*a good piece of one continent / and another continent*), after an outburst of frustration (*the whole damned thing!*) and a dead-end reference (*He who loseth his life, etc.*), after an outburst of uncontainable grief and citation from Lear (*neever[sic], no never never never again*), the top-heavy "primitive column" now teetering on its frail footing of keys, glasses, and pens, construction stops. But another column is forming in the margin,

A　　a
X　　b
B　　a

the refrain and rhyme patterns for a villanelle, plus the number 6 (six words needed for X) and some endword candidates: *ever/ never/forever; geography/scenery/-ly/easily/instinctively; intelligent/continent/spent/sent/lent/evident.*

So far, nothing here necessarily contradicts either Wordsworth or Heaney: the page is full of hesitancies, approaches; the marginalia are primarily musical (one line of iambic pentameter, clearly added later, sets the cadence, and the traditional form will organize it). If the biographers are right, however, and the blue eyes are Alice Methfessel's, the grief breaking through the poet's tranquillity is less recollected (Lota de Macedo Soares's suicide) than anticipated. But neither Wordsworth nor Heaney nor Bishop's biographers can quite translate for the general reader the extent to which the working poet sees, in initial drafts, a formal challenge. The essential problems presented by this draft center on tone—which now yaws from flip to anguished, from sarcastic to maudlin—and the high degree of repetition, born of obsession and itself generative but spinning the poem out of control. Bishop's response: the discipline of an existing traditional form that converts reiteration into refrain. Whereby "the structure changed from a column to an arch, bending off in a smooth curve, [and] the arch was joined." By the next draft Bishop is committed to the villanelle with a secure opening (and recurrent) line: *The art of losing isn't hard to master.* Now the work will have purpose and focus, building the nest's interior, the "three-dimensional maze, intricate arrangements of spiraling galleries, corridors, . . . arched vaults, . . . great caverns."

But doing so will take at least six months and fifteen drafts. In them Bishop seems not so much laboring "to articulate sweet sounds together," transliterating epiphany, as journeying toward a moment of vision, of insight, that would accommodate Coleridge's "reconciliation of opposites"—the two extremes here being the tight-lipped self-dismissive tone of the opening line and the casual quotidian detail on the one hand, and on the other the unspeakable fear and self-reproach that swamped the earliest efforts at the poem. Bishop does not seek entry at the point closest to the emotion; rather, as Brett Millier reports, the next two drafts "work mostly on the first four stanzas, whittling the catalog of losses into a discreet and resonant form and setting the rhyme scheme firmly" (*Elizabeth Bishop: Life and the Memory of It*). In the fifth and sixth drafts Bishop's focus is on the final stanza, again breaking under the weight of the tonal shift:

The art of losing's not so hard to master
But won't help in think of that disaster

No—I am lying—

(Draft 5)

The art of losing's not so hard to master
until that point & then it
fails & is disaster—

(Draft 6)

Draft 7 stops short of the final stanza, and draft 8 seems to undo previous work, severely, with a new opening tercet (compressing the earlier nine lines into three) and end-word schema, and a start at closure with most of the lines crossed out.

Millier assumes that "some time passed between the eighth and ninth drafts, for all the later attempts . . . contain completed versions of all six stanzas." Unresolved in the interim was the poem's epiphany and resolution, that bridge from the least trivial (*continent*) to the most significant (the beloved), from supportable to unsupportable. What's achieved in draft 9 is a firm structure. Although the exact wording (even the end words) will vary before she's through, the architecture—the development of the argument within the refrain—is secured and will not, from here on out, be doubted:

stanza 1: willingness *to be lost* residing within things
stanza 2: first imperative and *usual list*: *Lose something every day* (keys, glasses)
stanza 3: second imperative and return to the metaphor of the title (*Practice losing . . .*)
stanza 4: intensified tone (*Look!*) and increased value of lost items (mother's watch, houses)
stanza 5: *vaster losses*, cities, a continent

It seems not farfetched to think that this structural solidity, and the arc of the steadily torqued tone, precipitate another timely arch, the first promising sketch of a final stanza:

All that I write is false, it's evident
The art of losing isn't hard to master.

oh no.
[anything] at all anything but one's love. (Say it: disaster.)

Something is solved there with Bishop's characteristic parenthesis. (I have restored *in brackets* what she crossed out in the various drafts.) It enables a return of the hard-nosed, intrusive voice of draft 1 (also parenthetical) which articulates the other side—the underside—of the paradox, and its appearance supplies a crucial structural piece, clarified in the immediate adjustment written and crossed out in draft 10, restored in 11—

The art of losing wasn't hard to master
with one exception. (<u>Write it.</u>) Write "disaster"—

and then stewed over in draft 12:

the art of losing wasn't too hard to master
with this exception. (Stupid! Write!)
                    (<u>Write it!</u>) this disaster.
except this loss (<u>Oh, write it!</u>) this disaster.
but this loss is (Go on: write it!) is [seems] disaster.

This art of losing wasn't too hard to master
in general, but his (Oh, write it!)   seems
in general, but this (Oh go on! Write it!) looks like disaster.
but this (Oh go on! Write it!) seems disaster.
doesn't (oh isn't it) it does look like disaster—

By draft 13 the stutter is secured, emphasis and quotation marks replaced by extended syntax and alliteration: a return of the recurrent *L* of *lose, losing, lost, last, lovely,* and *love*:

even if this [when it] looks like (Write it!) like disaster.

Now again revision becomes purposeful, still focused on tone, the remaining extant drafts seeming to work backward from that authority. As if to establish the ground to be violated by the interruption, the changes in the refrain (drafts 13 and 14) move away from assertion and certainty toward ambivalence:

> the loss of love is possible to master,
> 　　　　　. . . something one must master
> 　　　　　. . . not too hard to master . . .

Meanwhile, after Bishop restores, in draft 10, the specific "you" of the initial draft, there is a similar movement in diction:

> But, losing you (eyes of the Azure Aster)
> And losing you now (a special voice, a gesture)
> 　. . . (a funny voice . . . the joking voice)

What remains unresolved, however, and stubborn, is the exact amount of self-knowledge in the controlling voice. Draft 10's "I've written lies above" is changed in pencil to "above's all lies," the two phrases then alternating with "I wrote a lot of lies" through five reworkings of the stanza in draft 11—surviving in some form, that is, until its outright contradiction: in 12, *above's not lies* and then, through four reworkings, *I haven't lied above*; in 13, *doesn't mean I've lied [I'm lying]*; in 14, *these are not lies* (by hand). At the same time, each of the typed versions, 9–13 makes some small change to the wording of the first five stanzas—final editorial adjustments concomitant with the large-scale wrestling with the conclusion.

　　A carbon of the typed draft 15 is what Bishop sent to her friend the poet Frank Bidart for his response, but she was still fiddling with that closure (see Figure 2). His notes record the changes, written by hand, that she dictated to him over the telephone: "further" made "farther," in stanza 3; a dash to introduce stanza 6 ("—Even losing you"); "the" instead of "a" joking voice in that same line; and perhaps more significantly, elimination of the one full repetition in b, the rhyme that ends each tercet's variant middle line—a change, in line 2, from *so many things seem really to be meant* / *to be lost* to

> so many things seem filled with the intent
> to be lost that their loss is no disaster.

ONE ART

The art of losing isn't hard to master: ~~intent~~   *spilled with the intent*
so many things seem ~~really to be meant~~
to be lost that their loss is no disaster.

Lose something every day. Accept the fluster
of lost door-keys, the hour badly spent.
The art of losing isn't hard to master.

Then practice losing farther, losing faster:
places, and names, and where it was you meant
to travel. None of these will bring disaster.

I lost my mother's watch. And look! my last, or
next-to-last of three loved houses went.
The art of losing isn't hard to master.

I lost two cities, lovely ones. And, vaster,
some realms I owned, two rivers, a continent. ·
I miss them, but it wasn't a disaster.

— Even losing you (a joking voice, a gesture
I love) these ~~were~~ not lies⸺ It's evident
the art of losing's not too hard to master
though it may look like (Write it!) like disaster.

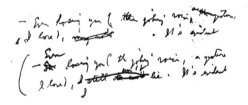

Maybe this small accommodation at the poem's opening simply diverted the poet's gaze long enough for a corrected final stanza to shimmer in peripheral vision. Or maybe the addition of another *L* word (*filled*) to line 2's torqued enjambment, without subsequent caesura, suggested a solution for closure as well. In any case, the fluster at the penultimate moment recorded by Bishop's hand on draft 15—*may not* (scratched through), *I [still do] [can't] [won't] lie*—finds resolution during the conversation with Bidart: annotating the typescript *these are not lies*, his notes first replace *are* with *were*, then restore *are* and enter *I shan't have lied*, a grammatical shift that nails the tone with future perfect tense.

The new helping verb, *shan't*, one should note, is placed in a position of stress, making a half rhyme on the stable b end sound (*intent, meant, went*), and marks an elevation in diction exactly counter to the movement toward idiom characteristic of all her other changes to the stanza. In that sense, it is an almost purely technical solution which yet embodies, within the tightly orchestrated music of the *L* verbs (*losing, love, lied*) and long vowels (*I, lied*), the tension between form and idiom—and thereby between inconvenience and assault, irritation and grief, mastery and disaster. And when it occurs, pushing the dramatic occasion into an imagined completed future, the emotional dilemma and the poem's true subject—anticipatory, unbearable dread—are suddenly, horribly clarified.

The question Bidart remembers her asking was whether it strayed too far from spoken idiom. His reassurance must have been sufficient, for the new phrase had already been added when the poem was set in type on April 26, 1976, six months after Millier dates the first draft, to recapitulate and just sufficiently overstate the ironic argument. Here is the "formidable edifice" in its published form:

One Art

The art of losing isn't hard to master;
so many things seem filled with the intent
to be lost that their loss is no disaster.

Lose something every day. Accept the fluster
of lost door keys, the hour badly spent.
The art of losing isn't hard to master.

Then practice losing farther, losing faster:
places, and names, and where it was you meant
to travel. None of these will bring disaster.

I lost my mother's watch. And look! my last, or
next-to-last, of three loved houses went.
The art of losing isn't hard to master.

I lost two cities, lovely ones. And, vaster,
some realms I owned, two rivers, a continent.
I miss them, but it wasn't a disaster.

—Even losing you (the joking voice, a gesture
I love) I shan't have lied. It's evident
the art of losing's not too hard to master
though it may look like (*Write it!*) like disaster.

Now what bridges the gulf into the final quatrain is one last
moment of dignified composure before heartbreak erupts from
underground. How account for that last crucial revision? Was
it Dionysian, an unstoppable continuation of the direct emotion (*gesture / I love*) acknowledged openly, finally, in draft 14?
Apollonian, derivative of the formal choice of severe enjambment, late caesura, alliteration? Occasioned by biographical circumstance, something Alice did or said, some small achievement
in that autumn's struggle with booze? Prompted by a suggestion
from Frank Bidart over the phone? All of the above? The point
remains: it took Bishop fifteen distinct drafts, another several

dozen alterations thereon, long deep thought in musical language, and impressive tenacity to arrive there, THERE being precise feeling and felt intelligence.

A long way from the Hollywood studio, but not that far, finally, from Coleridge in his study:

> In Shakespeare's poems the creative power and the intellectual energy wrestle as in a war embrace. Each in its excess of strength seems to threaten the extinction of the other. . . . What then shall we say? even this: that Shakespeare, no mere child of nature; no automaton of genius; no passive vehicle of inspiration possessed by the spirit, not possessing it; first studied patiently, meditated deeply, understood minutely, till knowledge, become habitual and intuitive, wedded itself to his habitual feelings, and at length gave birth to that stupendous power. (*Biographia Literaria*)

Selected Bibliography

Abrams, M. H. *The Mirror and the Lamp*. New York: Oxford University Press, 1953.

Aristotle. *Poetics*. Reprinted in *Criticism: The Major Statements*, ed. Charles Kaplan. New York: St. Martin's, 1986.

Auden, W. S. *The Dyer's Hand*. New York: Vintage, 1962.

Bayley, John. "Richly Flows Contingency." *New York Review of Books*, August 15, 1991, 3–4.

Berryman, John. *77 Dream Songs*. New York: Farrar, Straus & Giroux, 1964.

Bishop, Elizabeth. *The Complete Poems*. New York: Farrar, Straus & Giroux, 1969.

———. *Geography III*. New York: Farrar, Straus & Giroux, 1976.

Bogan, Louise. *The Blue Estuaries: Poems 1923–1968*. New York: Ecco, 1977.

Bradford, Curtis B. *Yeats at Work*. New York: Ecco, 1978.

Brooks, Cleanth. *The Well Wrought Urn*. New York: Harcourt, Brace & World, 1947.

Brooks, Cleanth, J. T. Purser, and Robert Penn Warren. *An Approach to Literature*. 3d ed. New York: Appleton-Century-Crofts, 1952.

Chappell, Fred. *Earthsleep*. Baton Rouge: Louisiana State University Press, 1980.

Coleridge, Samuel. *Biographia Literaria*. Reprinted in *Criticism: The Major Statements*, ed. Charles Kaplan. New York: St. Martin's, 1986.

Darwin, Charles. *The Origin of Species*. New York: Collier, 1909.

Dennis, Carl. "Mid-Course Corrections: Some Notes on Genre." Warren Wilson College, Swannanoa, NC, January 1997.

Dickey, James. *Drowning with Others*. Middletown, CN: Wesleyan University Press, 1962.

Dickinson, Emily. *The Complete Poems*. Cambridge, MA: Harvard University Press, 1955.

Dobyns, Stephen. *Black Dog, Red Dog*. New York: Holt, Rinehart & Winston, 1984.

———. *Heat Death*. New York: Atheneum, 1980.

Eliot, T. S. *Collected Poems, 1909–1962*. New York: Harcourt, Brace & World, 1963.

———. *The Sacred Wood: Essays on Poetry and Criticism*. New York: Methuen, 1920.

———. *Selected Essays*. New York: Harcourt, Brace & World, 1960.

Elizabeth Bishop and Her Art. Ed. Lloyd Schwartz and Sybil P. Estess. Ann Arbor: University of Michigan Press, 1983.

Ellmann, Mary. *Thinking about Women*. New York: Harcourt Brace Jovanovich, 1986.

Fitzgerald, F. Scott. *The Great Gatsby*. New York: Scribner, 1925.

Frost, Robert. *Collected Poems and Plays*. New York: Library of America, 1955.

Gallagher, Tess. *Instructions to the Double*. St. Paul, MN: Graywolf, 1976.

Gilligan, Carol. *In a Different Voice: Psychological Theory and Wonen's Development*. Cambridge, MA: Harvard University Press, 1982.

Glück, Louise. *Descending Figure*. New York: Ecco, 1980.

———. *Proofs and Theories*. New York: Ecco, 1994.

Gunn, Thom. "Christopher Isherwood: Getting Things Right." *Threepenny Review*, Summer 1990, 5–9.

Hardy, Thomas. *Selected Poems of Thomas Hardy*. Ed. John Crowe Ransom. New York: Macmillan, 1961.

Hass, Robert. *Field Guide*. New York: Ecco, 1973.

———. *Praise*. New York: Ecco, 1979.

———. *Twentieth Century Pleasures*. New York: Ecco, 1984.

Hayden, Robert. *Angle of Ascent: New and Selected Poems*. New York: Liveright, 1975.

Heaney, Seamus. *Government of the Tongue: Selected Prose, 1978–1987*. New York: Farrar, Straus & Giroux, 1989.

————. *Preoccupations: Selected Prose, 1968–1978*. New York: Farrar, Straus & Giroux, 1980.

Hikmet, Nazim. *Selected Poetry*. Trans. Randy Blasing and Mutlu Konuk. New York: Persea, 1986.

Jarman, Mark. "Aspects of Robinson." *AWP Chronicle* 30.3 (1997): 31–34.

Jarrell, Randall. "Levels and Opposites: Structure in Poetry." *Georgia Review* 50.4 (1996): 697–713.

Jourdain, Robert. *Music, the Brain, and Ecstasy: How Music Captures Our Imaginations*. New York: Morrow, 1997.

Justice, Donald. *New and Selected Poems*. New York: Knopf, 1995.

Keats, John. *The Essential Keats*. Selected Philip Levine. New York: Ecco, 1987.

————. *The Letters of John Keats, 1814–1821*. Ed. H. E. Rollins. Cambridge, MA: Harvard University Press, 1958.

Kinnell, Galway. *The Book of Nightmares*. Boston: Houghton Mifflin, 1971.

Koch, Kenneth. *Wishes, Lies, and Dreams: Teaching Children to Write Poetry*. New York: Chelsea House, 1970.

Kunitz, Stanley. *Next to Last Things: New Poems and Essays*. Boston: Atlantic Monthly Press, 1985.

————. *The Poems of Stanley Kunitz, 1928–1978*. Boston: Little, Brown, 1979.

Langer, Susanne K. *Philosophy in a New Key: A Study in the Symbolism of Reason, Rite, and Art*. New York: New American Library, 1951.

Larkin, Philip. *The Collected Poems*. New York: Farrar, Straus & Giroux, 1989.

————. *Required Writing: Miscellaneous Pieces, 1955–1982*. New York: Farrar, Straus & Giroux, 1984.

Lauterbach, Ann. "The Night Sky IV." *American Poetry Review* 26.4 (1997): 35–41.

Levertov, Denise. *The Jacob's Ladder*. New York: New Directions, 1961.

Levine, Philip. *The Names of the Lost*. New York: Atheneum, 1976.

Lewontin, Richard. Reply to Letters to the Editors. *New York Review of Books*, March 6, 1997, 51.

The Literature of the South. Ed. Thomas Daniel Young, Floyd C. Watkins, and Richard Croom Beatty. Glenview, IL: Scott, Foresman, 1952.

Lux, Thomas. *Half-Promised Land*. Boston: Houghton Mifflin, 1986.

McGrath, Tom. "The Frontiers of Language." *North Dakota Quarterly* 50.4 (1982): 28.

McHugh, Heather. *A World of Difference*. Boston: Houghton Mifflin, 1981.

McPherson, Sandra. *The Year of Our Birth*. New York: Ecco, 1978.

Merrill, James. *A Different Person: A Memoir*. New York: Knopf, 1993.

Millay, Edna St. Vincent. *Collected Poems*. New York: Harper & Row, 1956.

Millier, Brett. *Elizabeth Bishop: Life and the Memory of It*. Berkeley: University of California Press, 1993.

Motion, Andrew. *Philip Larkin: A Writer's Life*. London: Faber & Faber, 1993.

Mueller, Lisel. *Second Language*. Baton Rouge: Louisiana State University Press, 1986.

Murray, Gilbert. *The Classical Tradition in Poetry*. Cambridge, MA: Harvard University Press, 1930.

The Norton Anthology of Literature by Women. Ed. Sandra Gilbert and Susan Gubar. New York: Norton, 1985.

O'Connor, Flannery. *The Complete Stories*. New York: Farrar, Straus & Giroux, 1971.

————. *The Habit of Being: Letters of Flannery O'Connor*. Ed. Sally Fitzgerald. New York: Farrar, Straus & Giroux, 1979.

————. *Mystery and Manners*. Ed. Sally Fitzgerald. New York: Farrar, Straus & Giroux, 1979.

Oliver, Mary. *Dream Work*. Boston: Atlantic – Little, Brown, 1986.

Orr, Gregory. *We Must Make a Kingdom of It*. Middletown, CN: Wesleyan University Press, 1986.

Ostriker, Alicia Suskin. *Stealing the Language*. Boston: Beacon, 1986.

Pinker, Steven. *The Language Instinct: How the Mind Creates Language*. New York: Harper Perennial, 1995.

Pinsky, Robert. *The Situation of Poetry*. Princeton, NJ: Princeton University Press, 1976.

Plath, Sylvia. *The Collected Poems*. New York: Harper & Row, 1981.

————. *Johnny Panic and the Bible of Dreams, and Other Prose Writings*. London: Faber & Faber, 1977.

Plato. *Republic*. Trans. Alan Bloom. New York: Basic Books, 1968.

Pound, Ezra. *Selected Prose, 1909–1965*. Ed. William Cookson. New York: New Directions, 1973.

The Princeton Encyclopedia of Poetry and Poetics. Ed. Alex Preminger. Princeton, NJ: Princeton University Press, 1974.

Ransom, John Crowe. "Wanted: An Ontological Critic," "An Address to Kenneth Burke," and "Positive and Near-Positive Aesthetics." In *Beating the Bushes: Selected Essays 1941–1970*, 1– 46, 47– 71, 72 – 79. New York: New Directions, 1972.

———. "Criticism as Pure Speculation." In *Selected Essays of John Crowe Ransom*, ed. T. D. Young and John Hindle, 128 – 46. Baton Rouge: Louisiana State University Press, 1984.

———. *Selected Poems*. New York: Knopf, 1963.

———. *The World's Body*. Baton Rouge: Louisiana State University Press, 1968.

Richards, I. A. *Practical Criticism*. New York: Harcourt, Brace, 1929.

Ritvo, Harriet. *The Platypus and the Mermaid and Other Figures of the Classifying Imagination*. Cambridge, MA: Harvard Univesity Press, 1997.

Roethke, Theodore. *The Collected Poems of Theodore Roethke*. Seattle: University of Washington Press, 1982.

Shakespeare, William. *The Complete Works of Shakespeare*. Ed. Hardin Craig. Glenview, IL: Scott, Foresman, 1961.

Southern Writing in the Sixties: Poetry. Ed. John William Corrington and Miller Williams. Baton Rouge: Louisiana State University Press, 1967.

Stallworthy, Jon. *Between the Lines*. New York: Oxford University Press, 1963.

Stevens, Wallace. *Collected Poems*. New York: Knopf, 1973.

Taylor, Eleanor Ross. *Days Going/Days Coming Back*. Salt Lake City: University of Utah Press, 1991.

Thomas, Lewis. *The Lives of a Cell*. New York: Viking, 1974.

Thompson, Lawrance, and R. H. Winnick. *Robert Frost: A Biography*. New York: Holt, Rinehart & Winston, 1982.

Thrall, William Flint, and Addison Hibbard. *A Handbook to Literature*. Rev. and enl. C. Pugh Holman. New York: Odyssey Press, 1960.

Warren, Robert Penn. *Selected Poems, 1923–1975*. New York: Random House, 1975.

Williams, William Carlos. *Selected Poems*. New York: New Directions, 1949.

Wordsworth, William. Preface to *Lyrical Ballads*. Reprinted in *Criticism: The Major Statements*, ed. Charles Kaplan. New York: St. Martin's, 1986.

Wright, Charles. *Bloodlines*. Middletown, CN: Wesleyan University Press, 1975.

———. *Hard Freight*. Middletown, CN: Wesleyan University Press, 1973.

Wright, James. *Collected Poems*. Middletown, CN: Wesleyan University Press, 1971.

Yeats, William Butler. *Essays and Introductions*. New York: Macmillan, 1961.

———. *Selected Poems*. New York: Macmillan, 1962.

Index

The Life of Poetry

POETS ON THEIR ART AND CRAFT

Sherod Santos, *A Poetry of Two Minds*

Ellen Bryant Voigt, *The Flexible Lyric*